FDI Qualities Review of Tunisia

BOOSTING PRODUCTIVITY AND CREATING BETTER JOBS

OECD
BETTER POLICIES FOR BETTER LIVES

This document was produced with the financial assistance of the European Union. The views expressed herein can in no way be taken to reflect the official opinion of the European Union.

Please cite this publication as:
OECD (2024), *FDI Qualities Review of Tunisia: Boosting Productivity and Creating Better Jobs*, OECD Publishing, Paris, https://doi.org/10.1787/d8a28bca-en.

ISBN 978-92-64-63160-1 (print)
ISBN 978-92-64-91848-1 (PDF)
ISBN 978-92-64-81715-9 (HTML)
ISBN 978-92-64-94791-7 (epub)

Photo credits: Cover © petrenkod/Getty Images

Corrigenda to OECD publications may be found on line at: www.oecd.org/about/publishing/corrigenda.htm.

Foreword

This *FDI Qualities Review of Tunisia* examines how foreign direct investment (FDI) can help Tunisia meet the Sustainable Development Goals (SDGs) in the areas of productivity and innovation, trade, employment and job quality, and skills development. FDI provides an important source of financing in Tunisia, but the reform momentum needs to be sustained and deepened so that the benefits of investment can be shared more widely across society and further contribute to Tunisia's ambition of becoming a knowledge-based economy. The review sheds light on the contribution of FDI to sustainable development using a wealth of national and international data sources and identifies policy directions to increase its positive impacts.

The review was prepared by the OECD in cooperation with the Tunisian Foreign Investment Promotion Agency (FIPA) and with the support of a dedicated taskforce that included the Ministry of Economy and Planning, the National Institute of Statistics, the Tunisian Investment Authority, the Agency for the Promotion of Industry and Innovation, and the Tunisian Institute of Competitiveness and Quantitative Studies. Guidance and support from FIPA, represented by Jalel Tebib and Imène Saadi, were instrumental to successful completion of the review. FIPA's Thouraya Khayati, Sami Bouselmi and Zied Lahbib provided additional guidance. Fathi Elhajamara, National Institute of Statistics, provided valuable statistics based on the *Répertoire National des Entreprises*.

This review is part of the OECD FDI Qualities Initiative and an output of the EU-OECD Programme on Investment in the Mediterranean. The FDI Qualities Initiative provides governments with the data, tools, and standards to assess the contribution of FDI to sustainable development and identify policies to increase its positive impacts. The EU-OECD Programme on Investment in the Mediterranean supports investment reform efforts that contribute to job creation and sustainable growth in the Middle East and North Africa region. This review builds on the longstanding cooperation between Tunisia and the OECD under the MENA-OECD Competitiveness Programme. Tunisia is an adherent to the OECD Declaration on International Investment and Multinational Enterprises and has completed an OECD Investment Policy Review in 2012. The Review was financially supported by the European Union.

The review was prepared by Paula Adamczyk, Economist, and Fares Al-Hussami, Head of FDI Qualities and Impact, Sustainable Investment Unit, Investment Division, Directorate for Financial and Enterprise Affairs, under the supervision of Martin Wermelinger, Head of Sustainable Investment Unit. Ana Novik and Stephen Thomsen, Head and Deputy Head of Investment Division, provided overall guidance. Stratos Kamenis, Economist and Project Manager, provided substantive inputs. Delegates of the OECD Investment Committee, FIPA's Sami Bouselmi, and ILO's Christoph Ernst, Martin Ostermeier, Joyanna Pelivani, and Reina Kuwashima provided valuable comments. The analysis also benefited from substantive discussions with Leila Baghdadi, World Bank, and Carl Daspect, Delegation of the EU to Tunisia. The review was approved by written procedure by the OECD Investment Committee on 27 May 2024. Lucinda Pearson, Communication Officer, prepared the report for publication.

Table of contents

FIGURES

TABLES

BOXES

Follow OECD Publications on:

https://twitter.com/OECD

https://www.facebook.com/theOECD

https://www.linkedin.com/company/organisation-eco-cooperation-development-organisation-cooperation-developpement-eco/

https://www.youtube.com/user/OECDiLibrary

https://www.oecd.org/newsletters/

Executive summary

Tunisia's small open economy has strongly benefitted from trade and investment openness and integration in global value chains (GVCs). Major business climate reforms, including in recent years, and the creation of the offshore regime in 1972, led Tunisia to attract large amounts of foreign direct investment (FDI). The FDI stock-to-GDP ratio of 85% is high compared to other emerging economies – but has been trending downwards. Economic drawbacks caused by the Global Financial Crisis, internal political disruptions, and the COVID-19 pandemic considerably impacted FDI, which have been generally decreasing since 2012. In 2022, FDI flows represented 1.5% of GDP, which is low relative to the 2.3% in the MENA region and to previous years. Trade intensity – the share of exports and imports in GDP – reached 111% in 2022, twice as high as the OECD average. Labour productivity, however, is modest and has declined since 2011 due to limited competition, partly due to significant state involvement in the economy, hindering investment dynamism. Gross fixed capital formation dropped to 16% of GDP in 2022 compared to 26% in 2010.

The contribution of FDI to sustainable development is important but could further boost productivity and better job creation

Stalling FDI in Tunisia can set back progress towards the Sustainable Developments Goals (SDGs), as foreign firms are likely to create many jobs, pay higher wages, be more productive and better integrated in GVCs. Of all private firms in Tunisia, 3.5% were foreign owned in 2022. These foreign firms generated 11% of revenues and employed 21% of formal private sector workers. Nearly one foreign firm out of four employs at least 50 workers, against 2% of Tunisian firms, and 6.5% have more than 200 employees. While large foreign firms are mostly textile, mechanical, electronics or automotive equipment manufacturers, smaller foreign firms are services providers, principally of scientific, technical, business or ICT activities. Half of the foreign firms are micro businesses, possibly Tunisian diaspora investors purchasing land for agriculture, building a house, or starting a small business in their region of origin – often rural areas, in contrast with foreigners that choose coastal urban hubs. The metropolitan area of Tunis hosted 67% of foreign firms and attracted more than half of non-energy FDI between 2013 and 2022.

The large contribution of FDI to sustainable development is inherently linked to Tunisia's offshore regime, created in 1972. Combined with major liberalisation reforms in the 1990s, Tunisia's offshore regime exports led to increased FDI and strong integration in GVCs. In 2021, foreign offshore firms, in majority European export-processing manufacturers, represented 79% of all foreign firms, a share close to 100% in the textiles and electric-electronic and household appliance industries. The offshore regime model has shown its limitations, however, with a dual economy characterised by large, low value-added, exports in an offshore sector that is unable to create jobs for the highly educated youth and a protected domestic sector. Furthermore, foreign offshore manufacturers are poorly integrated in the local economy – in 2021, they sourced only 30% of their inputs from domestic firms, limiting knowledge spillovers to Tunisian SMEs.

The contribution of FDI to job creation is large and one of the highest in the MENA region but is limited to low-skilled jobs. An abundant, young and skilled workforce had made Tunisia an attractive investment destination. In 2021, one out of five private sector employees worked in a foreign firm – 34% in manufacturing and 10% in services, among which 95% in foreign offshore firms; the number of workers in foreign firms has also doubled since 2005. Most job opportunities are in lower-skilled occupations, however, created by large foreign manufacturers exporters. Jobs created by foreign firms in services were less important but required more high-skilled workers, particularly in ICT, business, scientific and technical services – in all these sectors, foreign firms accounted for 24% to 44% of employment. Even if most of the jobs created are in manufacturing activities, job creation from FDI in services and in renewables has expanded in the past decade. Foreign firms provide more on-the-job training than Tunisian firms, which reflects multinationals' continual need to adapt to competitive international pressure through upskilling. The impact of FDI on gender outcomes is mixed. Most workers in foreign firms are women, and in proportions higher than in Tunisian firms, but these women are often in low-paid jobs in textiles or in the tourism sector.

Foreign investment is gradually shifting to more technology- and skill-intensive sectors but could further support productivity growth and improved living standards. At the national level, labour productivity of foreign firms decreased by 17% between 2010 and 2022, and, in 2022, foreign firms were between 40% to 50% less productive than Tunisian firms. They also paid only marginally higher wages. At the sectoral level, however, foreign firms were more productive and paid higher wages than their Tunisian peers in most sectors. The discrepancy in performance at the national and sectoral level is driven by a few sectors where foreign firms are less productive than their Tunisian peers. These sectors accounted for nearly half of foreign firms' total revenues and include primarily automotive equipment and electric-electronics offshore exporter assembling imported components and re-exporting them with little value-added, limiting productivity and knowledge spillovers. The combination of incentives to offshore exporters and the limited attractiveness of the onshore sector is partly behind the mixed impact of FDI on productivity and wages.

Targeted reforms can help enhance the contribution of FDI to a knowledge-based Tunisian economy: key policy directions

Tunisia has undertaken comprehensive business climate reforms over the past years to unlock private investment, including FDI, with the objectives of reducing the large financing gap, creating more and better jobs, and boosting aggregate productivity. The 2016 investment law, adopted after extensive consultations with public and private stakeholders, further liberalised investment, and other legislative reforms strengthened investor rights, created a more investor-friendly environment and narrowed the policy gap between foreign and domestic firms. A new foreign exchange bill – to be ratified by the Parliament – should ease international business dealings. The authorities have also taken steps to reduce dependency on the offshore regime to attract FDI and improve its impact on local development. Further reforms are needed to improve the contribution of FDI to productivity, innovation, and better job creation for the highly educated youth. Based on an assessment of FDI impact on sustainable development, policy directions include:

- **Improving policy coherence by aligning investment policy and promotion with Tunisia Vision 2035** and national plans aiming at making Tunisia a knowledge-based economy with human capital as a source of innovation. Institutional coordination is essential to achieve this goal.
- **Continuing efforts to reduce the dichotomy between the offshore and onshore regimes to expand investors' motives** beyond low value-added, low-wage, export-processing activities to more productive segments of the value chain and services sectors that create jobs for the highly educated job seekers.
- **Strengthening pro-competition reforms, including reducing barriers to foreign investment in relevant services sectors** such as business services and ICT, to unleash economy-wide productivity gains and support a more dynamic private sector that creates more and better jobs.
- **Establishing robust monitoring and evaluation mechanisms to assess the impact of FDI** on productivity, innovation, and labour market outcomes and anticipate foreign firms' skills needs.

1 Overview

This chapter provides an overview of Tunisia' current state of sustainable development challenges and analyses trends in inward FDI across sectors. It describes how foreign investment contributes to Tunisia's sustainable development objectives and provides a summary of Chapters 2 and 3 on the impact of FDI on productivity, innovation, job quality and skills development.

1.1. Foreign investment is a major source of financing that has recently stalled

Tunisia's small open economy has strongly benefitted from trade and investment openness and integration in global value chains (GVCs). Major business climate reforms, including in recent years, and the creation of the offshore regime in 1972 led Tunisia to attract large amounts of foreign direct investment (FDI). Inflows of FDI reached their peak in 2006 at USD 3.2 billion, representing more than 9% of the GDP at the time. The FDI stock-to-GDP ratio of 85% is high compared to other emerging economies – but FDI inflows have been trending downwards (Figure 1.1). Economic drawbacks caused by the Global Financial Crisis and political disruptions in the past decade considerably impacted FDI inflows into the country, which have been generally decreasing since 2012 despite showing some signs of recovery in 2017 and 2018. External shocks resulting from the COVID-19 pandemic in 2020 brought about an additional contraction of FDI inflows. In 2022, FDI flows represented 1.5% of GDP, which is low relative to the 2.3% in the MENA region and to previous years, but higher than the 0.9% recorded in 2021 during the COVID-19 crisis.

Figure 1.1. The contribution of FDI to the Tunisian economy is important but has recently stalled

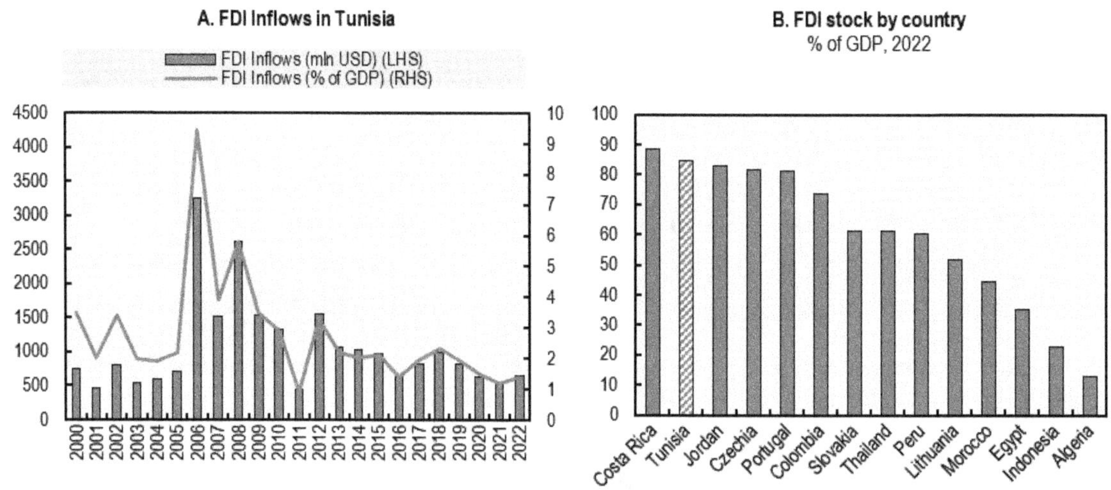

Source: (IMF, 2024[1]), IMF Balance of Payments Database; and (World Bank, 2024[2]), World Bank Developments Indicators.

Stalling FDI in Tunisia, together with sluggish economic growth, can set back progress towards the Sustainable Developments Goals (SDGs). Foreign investment helps reduce Tunisia's large external financing needs while foreign firms are likely to create many good jobs and boost productivity and innovation (OECD, 2022[3]). FDI can also help achieve Vision 2035, aiming at making Tunisia a knowledge-based economy with human capital as a source of innovation. Instability, with frequent changes in government affecting policy coherence and implementation, and uncertainty on priority reforms has slowed economic growth (Figure 1.2). This adversely affect business dynamism and contributes to the emigration of skilled youth. Recent geopolitical instability led to rising energy prices and persistent external imbalances (OECD, 2022[4]). GDP grew by less than 1% in 2023, compared to 2.6% in 2022, adversely affected by inflationary pressures, weighing on consumption and investment, and a decline in agricultural production. The Central Bank of Tunisia estimates GDP growth at 2.1% in 2024, considerably lower than the estimated growth of 3.9% in emerging economies on average (Central Bank of Tunisia, 2024[5]).

Figure 1.2. Economic growth in Tunisia has catch-up potential with other emerging economies

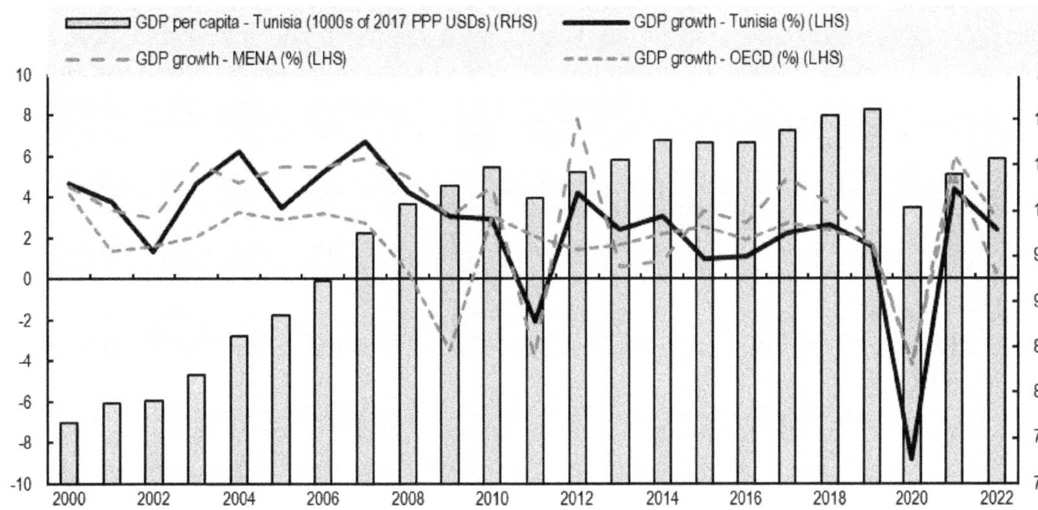

Source: (World Bank, 2024[2]), World Bank Developments Indicators; and (OECD, 2024[6]) OECD Economic Outlook database.

Despite ongoing challenges, Tunisia offers a variety of economic opportunities, including an educated workforce, a favourable geographical location, and free-trade agreements with the EU and Africa. The economy is diversified, with a large and increasing contribution of services to value added, a labour-intensive manufacturing sector, and an important agricultural sector relative to OECD countries (Figure 1.3). Trade intensity – the share of exports and imports in GDP – reached 111% in 2022, twice as high as the OECD average. Exports, particularly of machinery, electronics, textiles and clothing, have been important drivers of growth and job creation. Labour productivity, however, is modest by international standards and has even declined since 2011. Reallocation of capital to more productive sectors or segments of the value chains has been limited due to structural challenges, including significant state involvement in the economy, and weakened business confidence, hindering business dynamism (OECD, 2022[4]). Overall, gross fixed capital formation declined over the past decade and represented only 16% of GDP in 2022, compared to 26% in 2010, but has slightly increased since 2021.

Figure 1.3. Economic structure of Tunisia and comparator countries

Share of value-added by sector, in percent

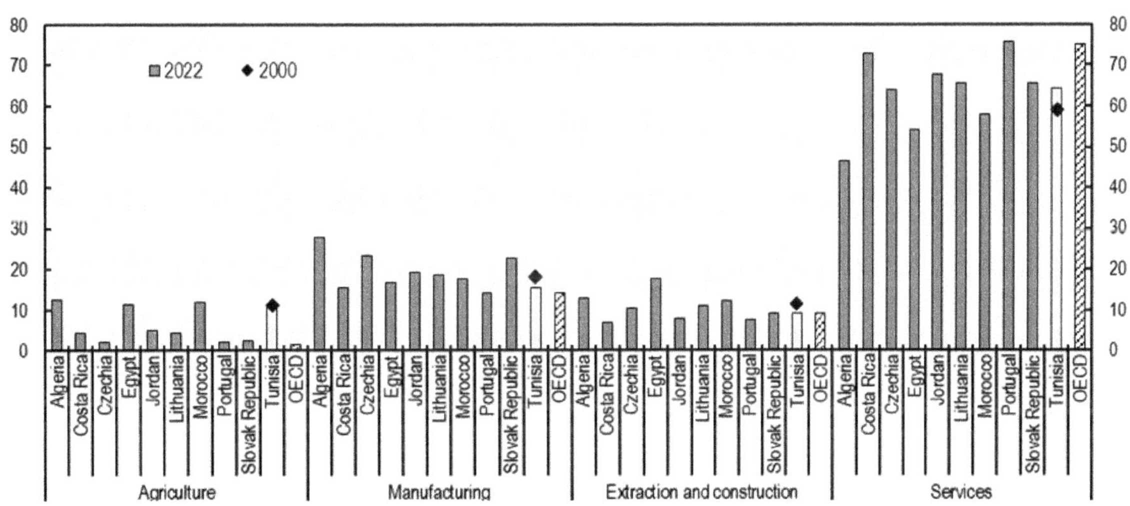

Source: OECD based on (World Bank, 2024[2]), World Bank Developments Indicators.

Tunisia has undertaken comprehensive business climate reforms over the past years to unlock private investment, including foreign investment. The 2016 investment law, adopted after extensive consultations with public and private stakeholders, further liberalised investment and introduced new incentives, including wage and training subsidies. Tunisia has since then continuously pursued legislative reforms to strengthen investor rights and create a more investor-friendly environment (OECD, 2021[7]). Little progress has been made since 2016 on streamlining restrictions on foreign ownership, however. The 2018 application decree of the investment law lists 243 authorisation and licensing regimes – authorisation is required to invest in 49 sectors if foreign ownership exceeds 50%. In sectors such as wholesale trade a blanket prohibition on FDI applies (OECD, 2021[7]; OECD, 2022[4]). Lowering barriers to foreign ownership in Tunisia's services sector such as business services, ICT, and transport and logistics could help unleash economy-wide productivity gains, including in export-oriented manufacturing activities relying on competitive and quality ICT infrastructure and services inputs, and confronted to increased fierce global competition (see Box 1.1).

Reforms also revamped the institutional framework for investment policy, although it is now composed of several bodies with partly overlapping mandates. The Foreign Investment Promotion Agency, FIPA, is responsible for the promotion and facilitation of foreign investment, similar to most investment promotion agencies (IPA) of OECD countries. With the ongoing geo-economic fragmentation, the agency focuses on providing competitive conditions to foreign investors considering nearshoring their operations to serve the large European market. FIPA operates under the umbrella of the Ministry of Economy and has several offices in Europe. The Tunisia Investment Authority (TIA) regulates investment activities and leads policy reforms in this area. It also provides tax incentives for large projects. The Agency for industrial and Innovation Promotion (APII) is responsible for promoting the industrial sector and innovation. It is the only investment body with subnational offices (OECD, 2019[8]). The presence of multiple agencies involved in investment issues generates considerable coordination needs to ensure policy coherence and delivery.

Tunisia is considering further reforms to enhance its investment framework: it has launched, in the context of its 2023-2025 National Reform Programme, a "National Strategy for the Improvement of the Business Climate", accompanied by a nationwide public e-consultation (OECD, forthcoming[9]). Ongoing reforms include a draft foreign exchange bill to ease international business dealings that was passed in March 2024 by the cabinet and is open for parliamentary review and ratification – foreigners face restrictions in making bank transfers abroad unless they are an offshore entity. By assessing the impact of FDI on productivity, innovation, quality job creation and skills development, this review provides additional policy directions for reforms than can help strengthen the contribution of FDI to sustainable development.

Box 1.1. FDI liberalisation in services can help unleash economy-wide productivity gains

Tunisia's trade and investment liberalisation efforts in the 1990s led to important FDI inflows (Figure 1.4, Panel A). However, regulatory restrictions on foreign ownership continue to be significantly higher than in OECD countries. Authorisation is required to invest in 49 sectors if foreign ownership exceeds 50% (Figure 1.4, Panel B). Restrictions on FDI also apply in several sectors, as set out by sector-specific and commercial legislations, among others, rather than consolidated in a negative list. They include foreign equity limits to acquisition and/or greenfield investments in agriculture, transport, telecommunications, financial services, wholesale and retail distribution, and media (Figure 1.4, Panel C). In tourism, foreign travel agencies may operate only indirectly through partnerships with Tunisian travel agencies (OECD, 2023[10]). FDI restrictions in services and infrastructure can hold back economy-wide productivity gains, including in manufacturing activities relying on competitive and quality services.

Figure 1.4. Regulatory restrictions on foreign ownership in Tunisia

FDI Regulatory Restrictiveness Index (FDIRRI), 2021

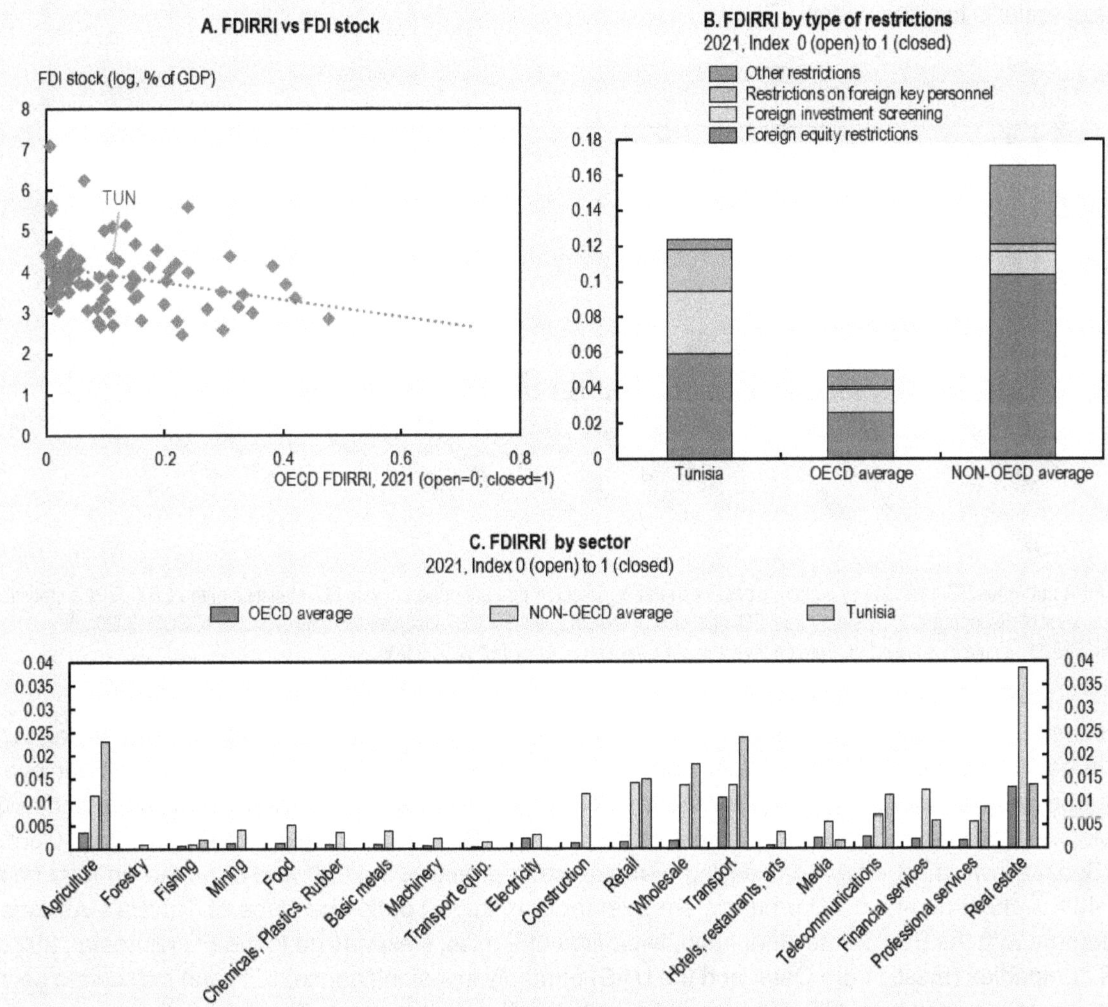

Source: OECD FDI Regulatory Restrictiveness Index (OECD, 2021[11]) https://www.oecd.org/investment/fdiindex.htm.

1.2. The contribution of FDI to sustainable development in Tunisia: main findings

1.2.1. Diversifying the sectors and sources of FDI can help improve economic resilience

The energy and manufacturing industries attract most foreign investments in Tunisia, although their importance has declined. In 2021, the energy sector attracted 29% of total FDI according to the latest available data from the Central Bank of Tunisia. Excluding the energy sector, and based on FIPA statistics, manufacturing has attracted the most FDI over the past decade (Figure 1.5). Manufacturing FDI more than doubled between 2013 and 2022 and about 75% of FDI in 2022 went to manufacturing, with the remaining directed at services, and less than 1% to agriculture. Within manufacturing, the electrics-electronics sector is the largest recipient, followed by chemicals, rubber, plastic and machinery and metals. The textile sector attracted only 3.5% of FDI. Services FDI has been concentrated in finance (38%), telecommunications (25%), and tourism and real estate (24%). The sectoral distribution of FDI in Tunisia is driven by many policy and non-policy factors, including privileges granted by the offshore regime to export companies and sectoral restrictions on foreign ownership in services sectors (OECD, 2021[7]).

Figure 1.5. Manufacturing is by large the first recipient of FDI followed by finance and ICT

Share of sector in total non-energy FDI

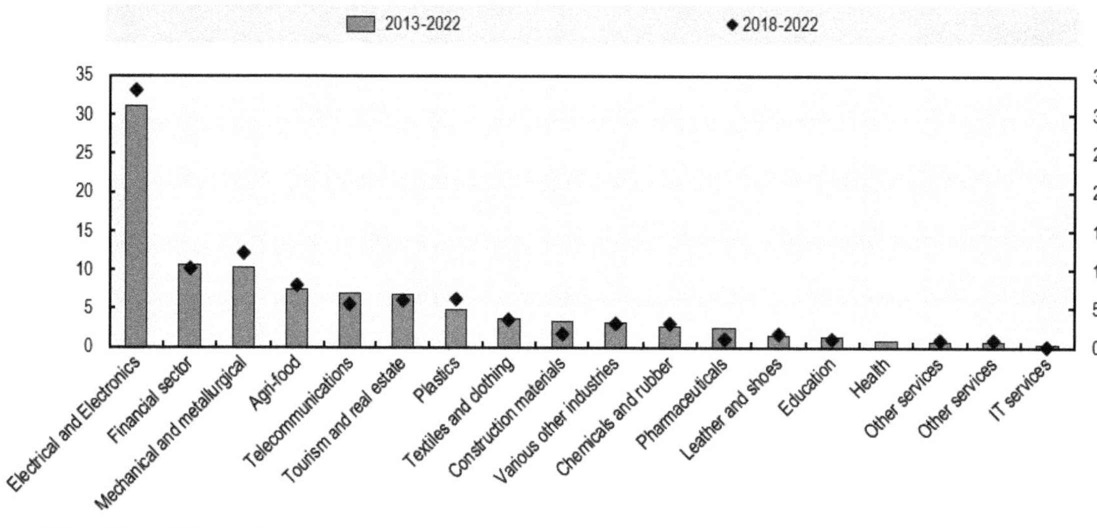

Note: FIPA publishes FDI statistics by sector, except for the energy sector, that are coherent with FDI statistics of the CBT. FIPA's statistics has a higher level of disaggregation by sector than FDI statistics of the CBT, but the CBT includes the energy sector (OECD, 2020[12]),
Source: OECD calculations based on Foreign Investment Promotion Agency (FIPA, 2023[13]).

Investors from the EU and the Gulf Cooperation Council (GCC) dominate the foreign investment landscape in Tunisia. Jointly, they held 84% of total non-energy FDI over 2013-2022. The two groups do not invest in the same sectors, with implications for the impact of the respective investments on various sustainable development outcomes (Figure 1.6). Investors from the EU (66%) – principally from France, Italy, Germany and Spain – own most export-processing manufacturing projects. In 2020, the EU share in total imports was 48% – most non-food EU products are exempt from import duties because of Tunisia's Association Agreement with the EU. On the other hand, two thirds of Tunisia's exports go to the EU (Eurostat, 2022[14]). GCC companies (mostly from Qatar and the UAE) primarily invest in finance, ICT, and real estate sectors, which are less export-oriented and geared towards the Tunisian market. Diversifying the sources of FDI would allow Tunisia to increase economic resilience to external shocks and global trade fluctuations.

Figure 1.6. EU investors are the largest in Tunisia but mostly invest in manufacturing

Total non-energy FDI over 2013-2022

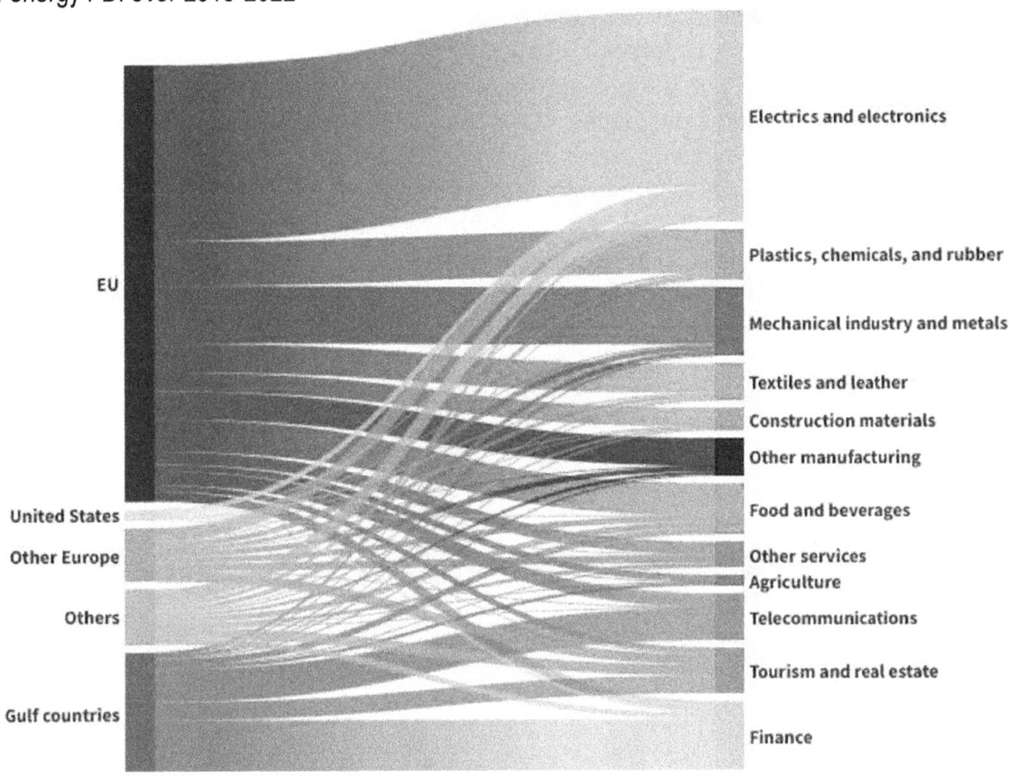

Note: Data excludes the energy sector.
Source: OECD calculations based on Foreign Investment Promotion Agency (FIPA, 2023[13]).

1.2.2. Many foreign firms are large export-processing offshore manufacturers

Stalling FDI in Tunisia can set back progress towards the SDGs, as foreign firms are significantly larger than Tunisian firms and, in turn, are likely to create many jobs, pay higher wages, be more productive and better integrated in GVCs. Benefits may not materialise automatically, however, and policies and institutional factors play an important role in enabling FDI direct and spillovers impacts. Realising this potential depends in large part on the type, motives, and sectors of foreign investment, as well as on the size, structure and technological advantages of the investing firm. The establishment of business linkages between foreign and Tunisian firms strongly depends on the capabilities of the latter (OECD, 2022[3]).

Of all private firms in Tunisia, 3.5% were foreign owned in 2022. These foreign firms generated 11% of revenues and employed 21% of formal private sector workers according to the *Répertoire National des Entreprises*. Nearly one foreign firm out of four employs at least 50 workers, against 2% of Tunisian firms, and 6.5% have more than 200 employees (Figure 1.8, Panel A). While large foreign firms – in terms of employment – are mostly textile, mechanical, electronics or automotive equipment manufacturers, many foreign firms are services providers, principally of scientific, technical, business or ICT activities (Figure 1.7, Panel B).

Half of the foreign firms are micro businesses, possibly diaspora investors purchasing land for agriculture, building a house, or starting a small business (Delahaye and Tejada, 2018[15]). The benefits of diaspora FDI may not be sizeable but are geographically more widespread. The Tunisian diaspora tends to invest in their region of origin – often rural or remote areas, in contrast with foreigners that choose major coastal urban hubs (UNDP, 2016[16]). Overall, the metropolitan area of Tunis – the Grand Tunis – hosted 67% of foreign firms and attracted more than half of non-energy FDI between 2013 and 2022 (Figure 1.7, Panel C).

The contribution of FDI to sustainable development is inherently linked to Tunisia's offshore regime, created in 1972. This regime grants exporting firms duty exemptions, tax incentives and preferential access to ports. Combined with major liberalisation reforms in the 1990s, Tunisia's model of economic growth, based on the offshore regime, led to increased FDI in low value-added exports and integration in GVCs. In 2021, foreign offshore firms, in majority export-processing manufacturers, represented 79% of all foreign firms, in stark contrast with Tunisian offshore firms that accounted for only 2% of Tunisian firms (Figure 1.7, Panel D). This share is close to 100% in the textiles and electric-electronic and household appliance industries. Tunisia's offshore regime, and related import-export activity, is dominated by EU investors.

Figure 1.7. Key characteristics of foreign firms in Tunisia

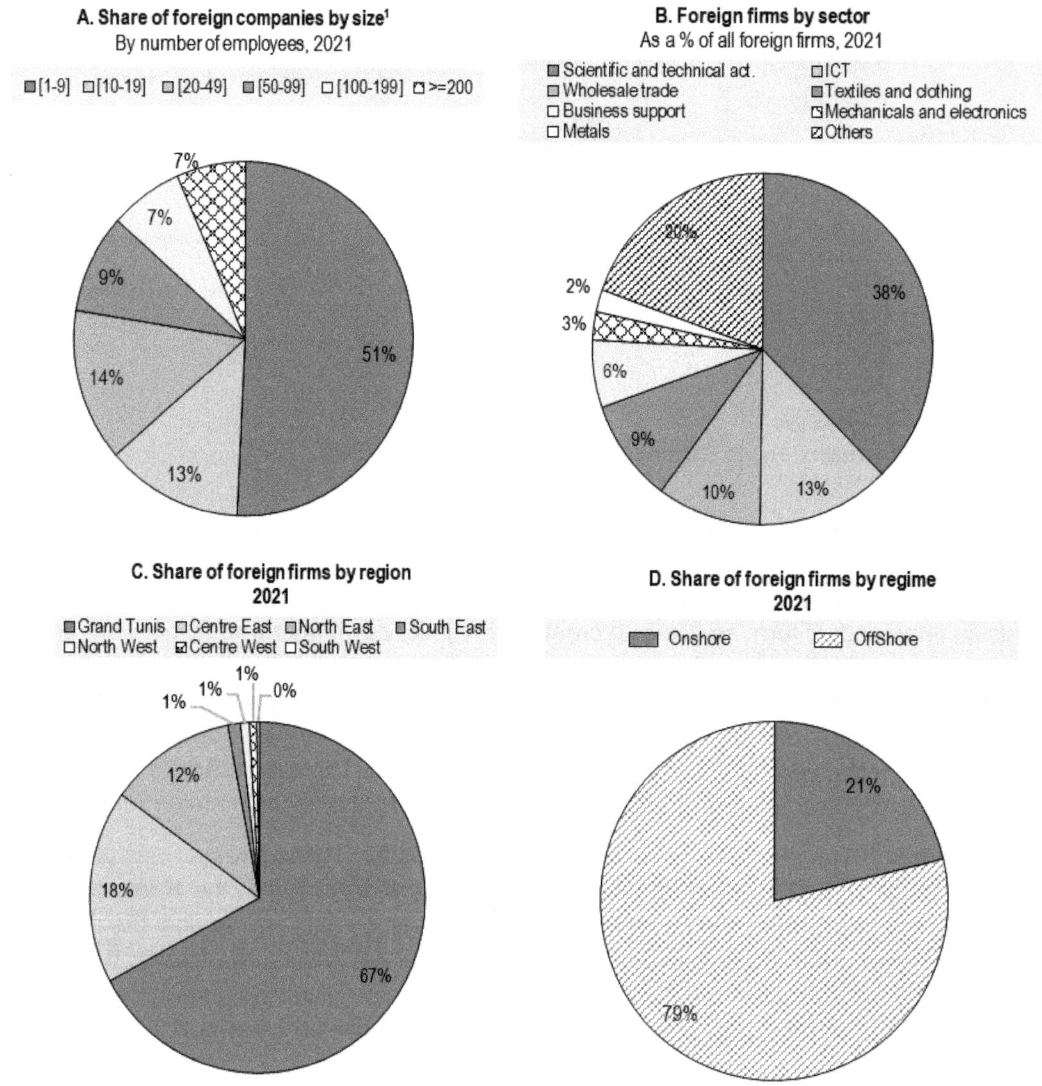

Note: 1. As a share of companies with at least 1 employee.
Source: OECD based on (INS, 2023[17]), Répertoire National des Entreprises.

Geared towards low value added, low cost production, the offshore regime model has shown its limitations, including its inability to create enough jobs for the highly educated youth entering the labour market

(Box 1.2). The economy became characterised by large, low value-added, exports in the offshore sector and a protected domestic sector (OECD, 2012[18]). Furthermore, foreign offshore manufacturers are poorly integrated in the local economy – in 2021, they sourced only 30% of their inputs from domestic firms, which is the lowest rate among MENA economies, limiting market opportunities and knowledge spillovers to SMEs (Joumard, Dhaoui and Morgavi, 2018[19]). Furthermore, offshore firms can sell a significant share of their goods on the domestic market, creating unfair competition with onshore firms. The authorities have taken steps to reduce dependency on the offshore regime to attract FDI and improve its impact on local development. Competitiveness in the onshore sector has improved with the liberalisation of key services, although further progress in this area would boost the attractiveness of the onshore regime to investment.

Box 1.2. Historical developments in Tunisia's offshore regime

At the beginning of the 1970s, Tunisia made a shift in its economic development policy and sought to involve foreign partners in its investment efforts. An offshore regime to encourage FDI was established, to attract low-cost production using unskilled labour. Exports of these offshore enterprises rose swiftly and the textile and clothing sector quickly overtook the oil industry. The share of fuel products in total goods export fell from 54% in 1981 to 16% in 1988. Electrical component exports also rose steadily.

With the promulgation of the Investment Incentives Code in 1993, strengthening the offshore regime, firms engaged wholly in export were eligible for numerous financial and tax advantages, including a total tax exemption for profits derived from export during the first 10 years. As in other countries such as Malaysia, which pursued a similar dual approach to development, the economy came to be characterised by rapidly growing exports and a protected domestic sector. Production for export was done primarily in enclaves and local value-added consisted essentially of low-cost and unskilled labour.

This approach may have been appropriate in the 1970s, given the country's education level and the preferences granted by Europe, but it began to show its limitations already in the 2000s, with the emergence of a new, educated and skilled generation of workers in the labour market. Offshore companies created many jobs, yet not enough to absorb an active population that rose considerably and included many university graduates entering the labour market for the first time. Furthermore, there was little effect on real wages and the system did not induce many indirect jobs by comparison with other forms of FDI that favour business linkages with local SMEs. Lastly, the favourable treatment accorded to the offshore sector came at the expense of the "onshore" sector (ILO, 2011[20])

The authorities have gradually been taking measures to overcome this dualism. Local and onshore firms have benefited from tariff reductions on imported components and cuts in corporate taxes. At the same time, offshore firms were gradually authorised to sell part their output on the local market (50% since 2011). Corporate income tax rates of the two regimes converged with the Budget law for 2021, although other tax privileges remain (OECD, 2022[4]). Competitiveness in the onshore sector has been improved with the liberalisation of key services such as banking and ICT. Further progress in this direction, making the services sector more open to competition and to foreign investors would boost the competitiveness of the onshore sector and help eliminate the distinction between these two sides of the economy, to the benefit of both.

Source: (OECD, 2012[18]), *OECD Investment Policy Reviews: Tunisia 2012*, OECD Investment Policy Reviews, OECD Publishing, Paris, https://doi.org/10.1787/9789264179172-en.

1.2.3. The contribution of FDI to employment is high but favours low-skilled jobs

An abundant, young and skilled workforce had made Tunisia an attractive investment destination. In 2021, one out of five private sector employees worked in a foreign firm – 34% in manufacturing and 10% in services, among which 95% in foreign offshore firms; the number of workers in foreign firms has also doubled since 2005. The large contribution of FDI to labour market outcomes is crucial for an economy confronted with high unemployment rates – 16% in 2023, particularly among youth, women, the educated workforce and workers in hinterland regions. As in other MENA countries, stalling business dynamism, combined with skills imbalances and labour market rigidities, has limited adequate employment opportunities for an increasingly educated Tunisian labour force (OECD, 2022[4]; ILO, 2023[21]).

Most job opportunities are in lower-skilled occupations, created by large foreign manufacturers exporting automotive components, textile and clothing, and mechanical and electronics products (Figure 1.8, Panel A). While the textiles and clothing industry is the largest private employer, both by foreign and Tunisian firms, it is the automotive equipment industry that counts the largest share of foreign firms employing the bulk of workers within the sector (Figure 1.8, Panel B). Jobs created by foreign firms in services were less important but required more high-skilled workers, particularly in ICT, business, scientific and technical services – in all these sectors, foreign firms accounted for 24% to 44% of employment. Demand for these higher-skilled jobs is stronger in the capital. Despite attracting half of FDI, jobs created by foreign firms in the metropolitan area of Tunis – the Grand Tunis – represented 28% of all FDI jobs, compared to 34% for the coastal Northeast region, where projects require less skilled workers but are more labour-intensive.

Figure 1.8. Foreign firms employ many workers in manufacturing, ICT and business services

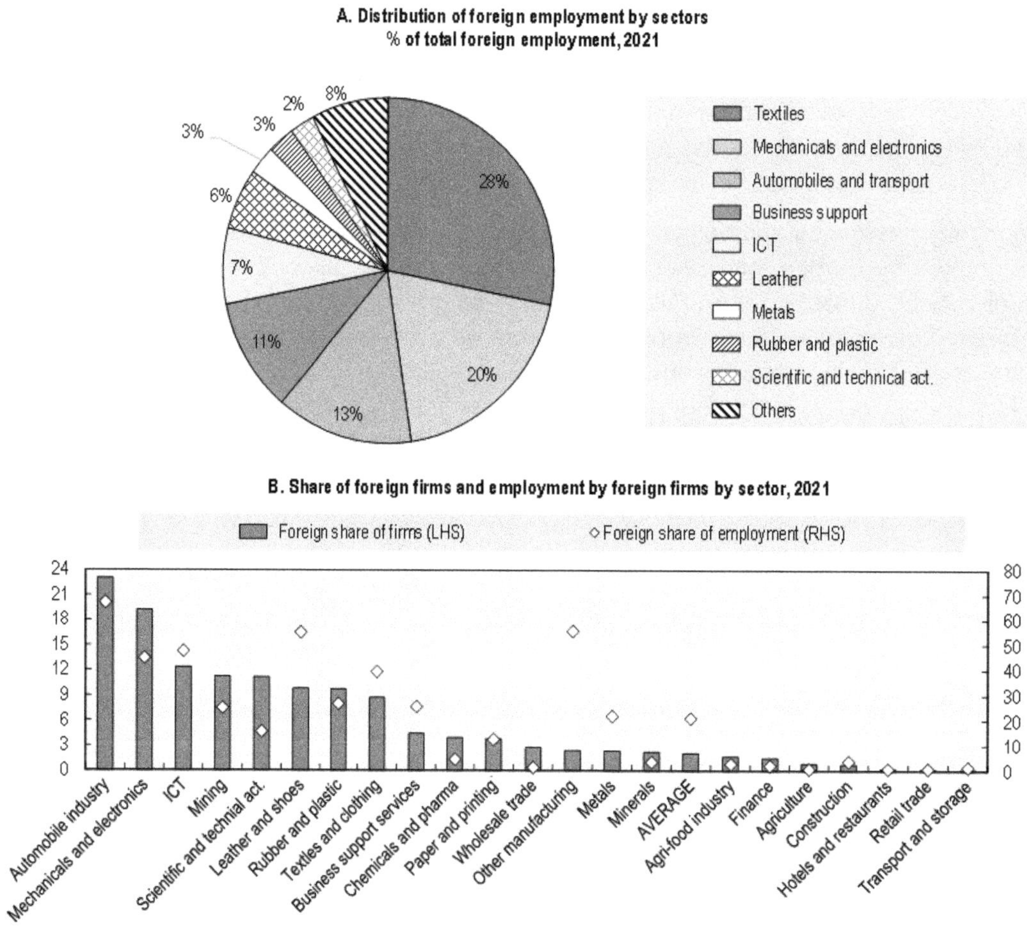

Source: OECD based on (INS, 2023[17]), Répertoire Nationale des Entreprises.

The job creation intensity of FDI in Tunisia is one the highest in the MENA region and significantly higher than the OECD average. It has also increased in the past decade, partly driven by a shift in FDI to job-creating assembling activities of the electronic components sector. Even if most of the jobs created are in manufacturing activities, job creation from greenfield FDI in services and in renewables has expanded in the past decade (Box 1.3) – EU greenfield investors created 66% of jobs in renewables. Business services, R&D, sales and marketing, which are activities that may better fit the educated young job seekers, contributed to 12% of new jobs created by greenfield FDI during 2013-23, twice more than in 2003-12. Total FDI – both greenfield and mergers and acquisitions – from the EU created 77% of all FDI jobs over 2012-2022, owing to labour-intensive manufacturing projects relative to GCC investors (Figure 1.9).

Figure 1.9. EU investors accounted for 77% of all jobs created by FDI between 2013 and 2022

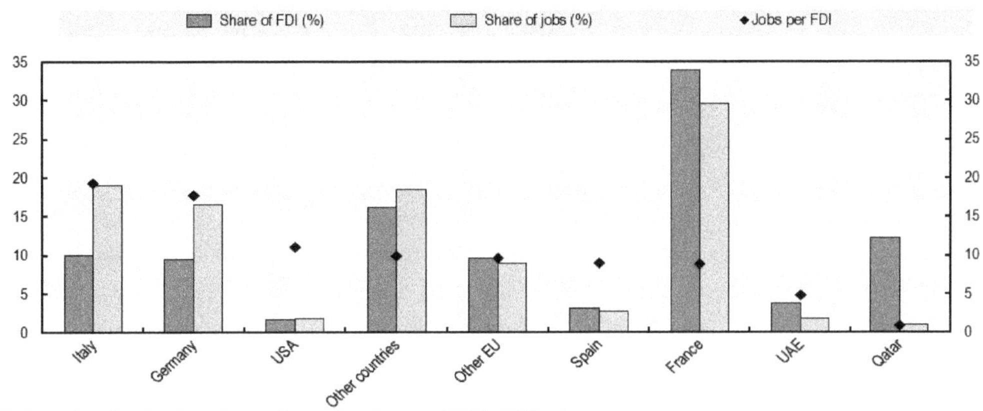

Source: OECD based on Foreign Investment Promotion Agency (FIPA, 2023[13]).

Foreign firms in Tunisia operate in a labour market with large skills imbalances – a misalignment between the demand and supply of skills, partly stemming from a high number of graduates, including many women, and low job creation for the highly skilled. Foreign firms have little impact on reducing this imbalance since their labour demand is geared towards low-skilled workers. Furthermore, they face severe skills mismatches, even more than Tunisian firms, as workers hired do not necessarily have adequate skills (Figure 1.10, Panel A). Hired workers are likely to be highly educated Tunisians constrained to accept jobs not corresponding to their qualifications, with adverse impacts on productivity. Foreign firms provide more on-the-job training than Tunisian firms, however, which reflects multinationals' constant need to adapt to competitive international pressure through upskilling (Figure 1.10, Panel B). The impact of FDI on gender outcomes is mixed. Most workers in foreign firms are women, and in proportions higher than in Tunisian firms, but these women are often in low-paid jobs in textiles or in the tourism sector (Figure 1.10, Panel C).

Figure 1.10. The contribution of foreign firms to skills development and gender equality in Tunisia

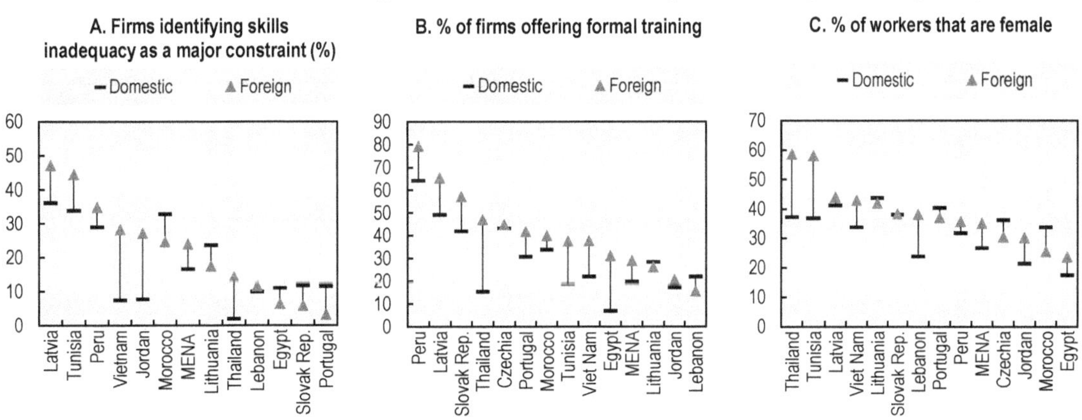

Source: OECD calculations based on (World Bank, 2024[22]), World Bank Enterprise Surveys (Tunisia: 2020), https://www.enterprisesurveys.org/en/data.

Box 1.3. Foreign investment in Tunisia's renewables sector can support a just green transition

Tunisia has abundant solar, wind and biomass resources. The government raised its renewable energy target from 30% to 35% by 2030 compared to the trend scenario in 2022. It also pledged to reduce its carbon intensity (emissions relative to gross domestic product) by 45% by 2030 compared to its 2010 level. There is no hydrogen strategy, but the government is working on establishing a new legal framework to promote the production and use of green hydrogen and its derivatives in the local market. Many solar equipment suppliers operate in Tunisia's solar market. Most of these entities can only manufacture and distribute equipment for small and medium solar projects. For large-scale solar projects, equipment tends to be imported (OECD, forthcoming[9]).

Foreign investment can play a fundamental role in supporting a just green transition in Tunisia. Globally, the share of renewable energy in total energy FDI expanded rapidly, reaching 84% in 2021. The shift of FDI in the energy sector away from fossil fuels and into renewables has consequences on job creation. Estimates show that, since 2019, jobs created from FDI in renewables even surpassed jobs from fossil fuel investments. In Tunisia, greenfield FDI in renewables strongly increased between 2003 and 2022 (Figure 1.11). Relatedly, jobs created from FDI in renewables represented 18% of all jobs created by FDI in the energy sector between 2013 and 2022 against only 4% between 2003 and 2012. EU greenfield investors created 66% of jobs in renewables over 2013-22.

Figure 1.11. Jobs created from greenfield FDI in renewables in Tunisia, 2003-2022

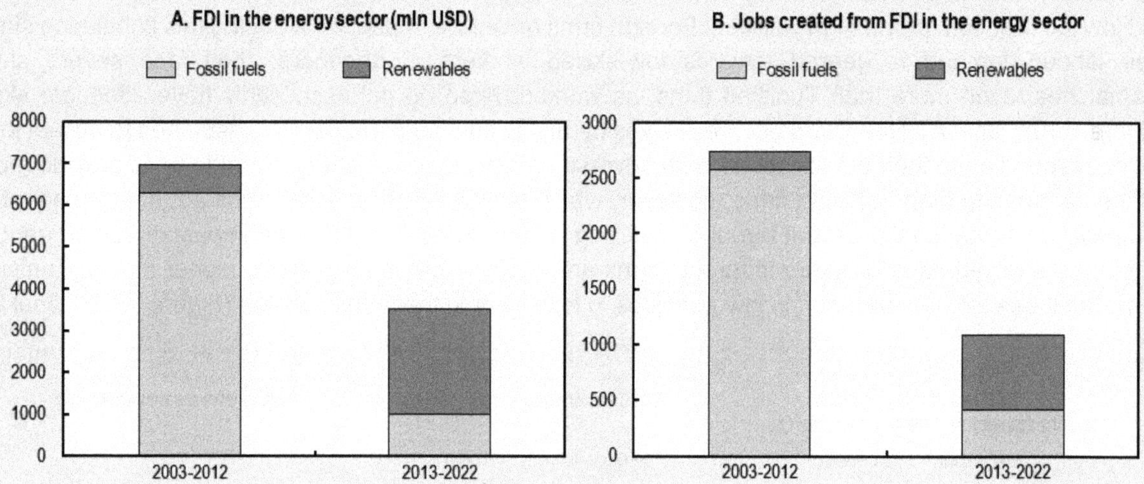

Note: Greenfield FDI corresponds to announced capital expenditure (CAPEX). Number of jobs and CAPEX are partly based on estimates.
Source: OECD calculations based on (Financial Times, 2024[23]) fDi Markets Database, https://www.fdimarkets.com.

In addition to supporting a just green transition, FDI can contribute to a decreasing carbon footprint thanks to the better overall environmental performance of foreign firms, particularly energy performance. Foreign firms in Tunisia perform better than domestic firms in terms of energy efficiency, measured as the amount of value added produced per unit input of energy. Furthermore, foreign firms are also more likely to use energy from their own renewable sources, monitor CO2 emissions across their supply chain or implement measures to reduce waste, thus being leaders of the green transition (OECD, 2023[24]).

1.2.4. The contribution of FDI to productivity and wages is limited but varies by sector

Foreign investment in Tunisia is gradually shifting to more technology- and skill-intensive sectors but could further support economy-wide productivity growth and improved living standards. At the national level, labour productivity of foreign firms decreased by 17% between 2010 and 2022, and, in 2022, foreign firms were between 40% to 50% less productive than Tunisian firms, depending on whether sectors with large informality are included or not (Figure 1.12, Panel A and B). They also paid only marginally higher wages. At the sectoral level, however, foreign firms were more productive and paid higher wages than their Tunisian peers in most sectors – productivity performance is often a catalyst for better wages (Figure 1.12, Panel C). The discrepancy in foreign firms' performance at the national and sectoral level is driven by a few sectors where foreign firms are largely present but are less productive than their Tunisian peers. Foreign firms' productivity and wage performances, relative to Tunisian firms, were higher in services than in manufacturing, but for productivity this performance has deteriorated in the past years.

Figure 1.12. Foreign firms are more productive and pay higher wages in most sectors

Foreign firms are more performant than Tunisian firms if the value is higher than zero

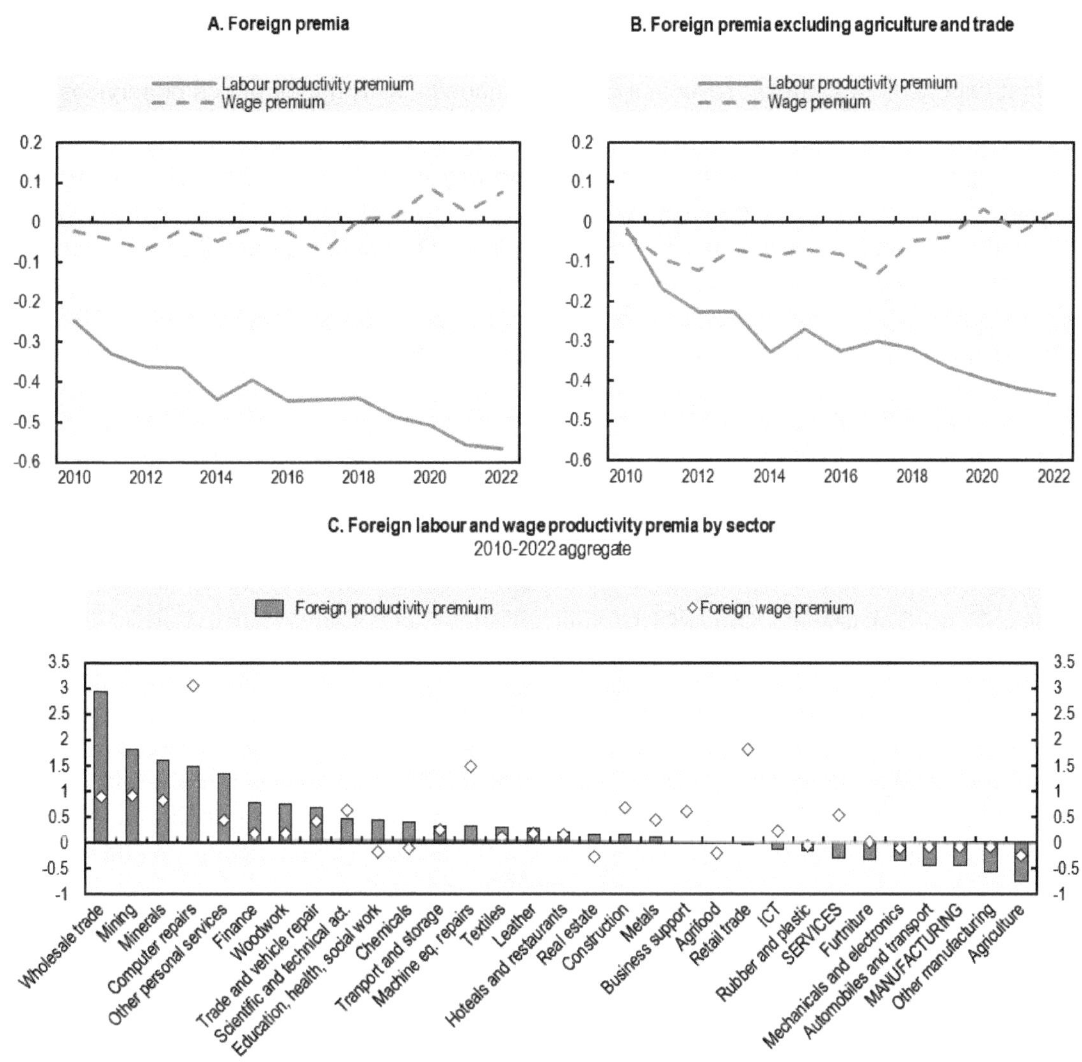

Note: Labour productivity is measured as revenues per employee. Panel B: the trade sector includes wholesale trade, trade and vehicle repair and retail trade, where levels of informal employment are high.
Source: OECD based on (INS, 2023[17]), the Répertoire Nationale des Entreprises sample.

The few sectors where foreign firms are less productive than their Tunisian peers accounted for nearly half of foreign firms' total revenues. They include primarily automotive equipment and electric-electronics offshore exporter and ICT firms. Foreign offshore exporters mostly assemble imported components and re-export them with little value-added, limiting productivity gains and knowledge spillovers. The ICT sector attracted the largest amount of services FDI over the past decade, after financial activities, and has the highest share of foreign firms in services (Figure 1.8, Panel B). But revenues of foreign ICT firms dropped sharply in 2019, while employment increased, leading to a decline in productivity. On the other hand, they paid higher wages than Tunisian firms. The textiles industry is one of the few large sectors where foreigners performed better, suggesting that their activities go beyond only processing or assembling.

The combination of incentives provided to offshore exporters and the limited attractiveness of the onshore sector, where FDI restrictions are high in productive sectors such as business and professional services, is partly behind the mixed impact of FDI on productivity and wages. From a policy perspective, it is less the foreign ownership of MNEs in Tunisia that drive their weak performance but rather that they operate in the offshore regime. The discrepancy between foreign productivity premia at the national and sectoral levels corroborates findings for offshore firms showing that productivity premia existed at the sectoral but not at the national level (Dhaoui, 2019[25]). Other findings show that offshore firms that are engaged in both exporting and importing underperform their onshore counterparts as they generally engage in processing and pure assembly activities (Baghdadi, Kheder and Arouri, 2019[26]). Finally, considering the significantly lower contribution of foreign firms to total revenues compared with employment (11% versus 20%), it is possible that exporters partly report revenues or profits made by selling their goods or services in foreign markets.

1.2.5. FDI supports Tunisia's ambitions of becoming a knowledge-based economy

Beyond supporting productivity enhancements in many sectors of the economy, FDI in Tunisia also supports innovation. Despite low levels of investment in R&D, technology diffusion from foreign firms contributes to improved innovation outcomes. Foreign firms are more R&D intensive than their Tunisian counterparts – 20% of foreign firms invested in R&D as opposed to 6% of Tunisian firms in 2021. Foreign firms are also more likely to introduce a product or process innovation but tend to be less innovative than in other comparator countries, partly as a result of their specialisation in less capital-intensive activities. The share of greenfield FDI going to R&D is smaller than in peer economies such as Portugal, Costa Rica or Lithuania. Little FDI goes directly to R&D activities, except in the ICT and the automotive sectors, which may help these sectors upgrade their production and export higher value-added goods and services and, in turn, improve their productivity. Sectors that are more R&D intensive, like pharmaceuticals, biotechnology, or medical devices do not attract much FDI (OECD, forthcoming[27])

1.3. Reforms can support FDI that boosts productivity and quality job creation: key policy directions

Enabling FDI that boosts productivity and creates quality jobs in Tunisia hinges upon a complex mix of policy measures that involve both a favourable investment policy environment and targeted policy reforms. An in-depth policy assessment for Tunisia is outside the scope of this review, but it could build on it to provide concrete reform suggestions and prioritise policy and institutional reforms to maximise the benefits of FDI on productivity and create more jobs. The OECD FDI Qualities Recommendation and related policy toolkit and principles could support such an assessment (Box 1.4).

Box 1.4. The OECD Recommendation on FDI Qualities for Sustainable Development

The Recommendation on FDI Qualities is structured around the following key high-level policy principles/directions, drawn from the FDI Qualities Policy Toolkit:

1. ***Governance:*** Provide coherent strategic direction on fostering investment in support of sustainable development, and foster policy continuity and effective implementation of such policies.
2. ***Domestic policy and legal frameworks:*** Take steps to ensure that domestic policy and legal frameworks support positive impacts of investment on sustainable development.
3. ***Financial and technical support:*** Prioritise sustainable development objectives when providing financial and technical support to stimulate investment.
4. ***Information and facilitation services:*** Facilitate and promote investment for sustainable development opportunities by addressing information failures and administrative barriers.
5. ***Development cooperation:*** Strengthen the role of development cooperation for mobilising FDI and enhancing its positive impact in developing countries.

The FDI Qualities Policy Toolkit is also structured along these policy principles/directions and provides detailed guidance to governments on enhancing the impacts of FDI in four areas of the SDGs, including productivity and innovation; job quality and skills; gender equality; and decarbonisation.

The Recommendation builds on other standards developed by the OECD in the area of international investment, including the Declaration on International Investment and Multinational Enterprises to which Tunisia adhered in 2012.

Based on this assessment of FDI impact on sustainable development, policy directions include:

- **Improve policy coherence by aligning investment policy and promotion goals with Tunisia Vision 2035 and national plans aiming at making Tunisia a knowledge-based economy with human capital as a source of innovation**. This implies a balanced approach towards job creation in investment policy that continues to target labour-intensive sectors, including outside of the Grand Tunis Area, while stepping up efforts to attract FDI in the digital economy and high-productivity, high-wage, services such as ICT, business services, and scientific activities. In manufacturing, supporting expansions in higher value-added activities of the automotive and electronics sectors can boost export sophistication, productivity, and skills spillovers, and could be more cost-effective than attracting new investors motivated by incentives of the offshore regime.
- **Continue efforts to reduce the dichotomy between the offshore and onshore regimes to** expand investors' motives beyond low value-added, low-wage, export-processing investments to more productive segments of the value chain and services onshore sectors that can match the large supply of highly educated job seekers. This includes reducing tax and regulatory differences, beyond corporate income tax, between the two regimes and stepping-up efforts to promote FDI outside of the offshore regime while improving the onshore regime's attractiveness, including by removing barriers such as the requirement for foreign investors to partner with Tunisian firms.
- **Strengthen pro-competition reforms to unleash economy-wide productivity gains and support a more dynamic private sector that creates more and better jobs.** Consider reassessing regulatory restrictions to foreign investment, notably horizontal restrictions and those in service sectors, such as business services, ICT, and transport, and, where relevant, streamline or remove them. Services restrictions can hold back economy-wide productivity gains, including in manufacturing activities relying on competitive and quality services. Foreign investment in services has also the potential to create jobs for both the low and highly-skilled Tunisian job seekers.
- **Establish robust monitoring and evaluation mechanisms to effectively assess the impact of FDI on productivity, innovation, and labour market outcomes**. This requires firm-level data, building on the Répertoire National des Enterprises (RNE), providing information on foreign

ownership, value-added, export, spendings on R&D and training, employment by gender, and labour costs. This necessitates improving coordination between the INS, FIPA, and APII. Consider involving FIPA and other relevant agencies in skill needs and anticipation exercises to design skills development programmes that target the needs of foreign firms.

References

APII (2024), *Tissu Industriel Tunisien*, http://www.tunisieindustrie.nat.tn/fr/tissu.asp. [28]

Baghdadi, L., S. Kheder and H. Arouri (2019), "Assessing the Performance of Offshore Firms in Tunisia", *Journal of Economic Integration*, Vol. 34/2, pp. 280-307, https://doi.org/10.11130/jei.2019.34.2.280. [26]

Central Bank of Tunisia (2024), *Périodique de Conjoncture N. 142 - Janvier 2024*, https://www.bct.gov.tn/bct/siteprod/documents/Conjoncture_fr.pdf. [5]

Delahaye, S. and G. Tejada (2018), "Transnational Investments of the Tunisian Diaspora: Trajectories, Skills Accumulation and Constraints", in *Contributions to Management Science, Diaspora Networks in International Business*, Springer International Publishing, Cham, https://doi.org/10.1007/978-3-319-91095-6_6. [15]

Dhaoui, S. (2019), *Offshore et productivité: Analyse économétrique à partir des données de l'enquête d'entreprises de la Banque Mondiale*, ITCEQ, http://www.itceq.tn/files/notes/offshore-et-productivite-2019.pdf. [25]

Eurostat (2022), *Tunisie: Voisinage du Sud*, https://neighbourhood-enlargement.ec.europa.eu/document/download/5b38ea77-9bdc-4ba5-844e-24593993cd15_en?filename=28032022-factograph_tunisia_fr.pdf. [14]

Financial Times (2024), *fDi Markets database*, https://www.fdimarkets.com. [23]

FIPA (2023), *Rapports annuels des IDE*. [13]

ILO (2023), *Impact des politiques de commerce et d'investissement sur l'emploi productif et décent: Rapport pays pour la Tunisie du projet « Intégration de l'Emploi dans le commerce et l'investissement dans le voisinage sud de l'UE»*, Organisation internationale du Travail – Genève : OIT, https://www.ilo.org/fr/publications/impact-des-politiques-de-commerce-et-dinvestissement-sur-lemploi-productif. [21]

ILO (2011), *Tunisia: A New Social Contract for Fair and Equitable Growth*, ILO Publishing, Geneva, https://www.ilo.org/publications/studies-growth-equity-tunisia-new-social-contract-fair-and-equitable-growth. [20]

IMF (2024), *Balance of Payments Database*, https://data.imf.org/?sk=7a51304b-6426-40c0-83dd-ca473ca1fd52. [1]

INS (2023), *Répertoire Nationale des Entreprises (RNE) database*. [17]

Joumard, I., S. Dhaoui and H. Morgavi (2018), "Insertion de la Tunisie dans les chaines de valeur mondiales et role des entreprises offshore", *Documents de travail du Département des Affaires économiques de l'OCDE*, No. 1478, Éditions OCDE, Paris, https://doi.org/10.1787/546dbd75-fr. [19]

OECD (2024), *Economic Outlook database.* [6]

OECD (2023), *FDI Qualities in the Middle East and North Africa: A mapping of policies and institutions that can strengthen sustainable investment*, Background document for the regional seminar on sustainable investment in the MENA region, OECD Istanbul Centre, https://www.oecd.org/mena/eu-oecd-mediterranean-investment/FDI-Qualities-MENA.pdf. [24]

OECD (2023), *OECD Competition Assessment Reviews: Tunisia 2023*, OECD Competition Assessment Reviews, OECD Publishing, Paris, https://doi.org/10.1787/a80cda01-en. [10]

OECD (2022), *FDI Qualities Policy Toolkit*, OECD Publishing, Paris, https://doi.org/10.1787/7ba74100-en. [3]

OECD (2022), *OECD Economic Surveys: Tunisia 2022*, OECD Publishing, Paris, https://doi.org/10.1787/7f9459cf-en. [4]

OECD (2021), *FDI Regulatory Restrictiveness Index*, https://www.oecd.org/investment/fdiindex.htm. [11]

OECD (2021), *Middle East and North Africa Investment Policy Perspectives*, OECD Publishing, Paris, https://doi.org/10.1787/6d84ee94-en. [7]

OECD (2020), *Examen par l'OCDE des statistiques d'investissement directs internationaux TUNISIE*, https://www.oecd.org/investment/Examen-par-l%E2%80%99OCDE-des-statistiques-d%E2%80%99investissement-directs-internationaux-Tunisie.pdf. [12]

OECD (2019), *Mapping of Investment Promotion Agencies: Middle East and North Africa - OECD*, OECD, Paris, https://www.oecd.org/investment/investment-policy/mapping-of-investment-promotion-agencies-med.htm (accessed on 27 February 2021). [8]

OECD (2012), *OECD Investment Policy Reviews: Tunisia 2012*, OECD Investment Policy Reviews, OECD Publishing, Paris, https://doi.org/10.1787/9789264179172-en. [18]

OECD (forthcoming), *Promoting investment and business climate reforms in Tunisia's pharmaceutical sector*, EU-OECD Programme on Investment in the Mediterranean. [27]

OECD (forthcoming), *Towards more sustainable investment frameworks: Evaluating the feasibility of Sustainable Investment Facilitation Agreements (SIFA) with Southern Mediterranean countries*, OECD Publishing, Paris. [9]

UNDP (ed.) (2016), *Case Study : Assessing the impact of diaspora investments in Tunisia*, https://www.undp.org/sites/g/files/zskgke326/files/publications/Case_Study_Assessing_the_impact_of_diaspora_investments_in_Tunisia.pdf. [16]

World Bank (2024), *World Bank Development Indicators database*, https://databank.worldbank.org/source/world-development-indicators. [2]

World Bank (2024), *World Bank Enterprise Surveys*, https://www.enterprisesurveys.org/en/data. [22]

2 FDI impact on productivity and innovation

This chapter examines the contribution of FDI to trade, global value chains (GVCs) integration, productivity and innovation. It analyses productivity differences between foreign and domestic firms at national and sectoral levels, and the extent of value chain linkages between foreign MNEs and Tunisian firms, an important channel of productivity spillovers. It also assesses the role of foreign firms in innovation and the local capacity of domestic firms, particularly small and medium-sized enterprises (SMEs), to benefit from the diffusion of knowledge and technology brought by FDI.

2.1. Summary

Tunisia's small open economy has benefitted from trade and investment openness and integration in global value chains (GVCs). The economy is diversified, with a large contribution of services to value added and a labour-intensive manufacturing sector. Manufacturing exports, particularly of machinery, electronics, textiles and clothing goods, have been an important driver of growth, but most economic activity is in low value-added activities and, in turn, labour productivity is modest by international standards and has even declined since 2011. Reallocation of capital to more productive sectors, including services, or higher value-added segments of the supply chains has been limited by structural challenges hindering investment and business dynamism, while global and domestic turbulences have weakened business confidence.

Private investment, especially foreign direct investment (FDI), could further contribute to economy-wide productivity growth and innovation in Tunisia. Foreign firms are more productive than their Tunisian peers in most sectors, including chemicals, finance, and mining – all large recipients of FDI. At the national level, however, foreign firms were 43% less productive than Tunisian firms in 2022. The few sectors where foreign firms are less productive accounted for 45% of foreign firms' revenues and are dominated by automotive and electric-electronics manufacturers operating in the offshore regime – the electric-electronics sector attracted the bulk of FDI in the past decade. Foreign exporters in the two sectors mostly assemble imported components and re-export them with little transformation and interaction with Tunisian suppliers, limiting productivity gains and knowledge spillovers from FDI. Overall, foreign firms purchase 30% of their inputs on the Tunisian market, which is lower than in other southern Mediterranean countries.

The productivity performance of foreign relative to Tunisian firms in services is higher than in manufacturing but has deteriorated over the past years. Foreign firms are more productive than Tunisian firms in all services sectors, except in ICT. The ICT sector attracted the largest amount of services FDI between 2013 and 2022, after financial activities, and has the highest number of foreign firms in services (12% of all foreign firms). Foreign firms' revenues in ICT have dropped sharply since 2019, however, while employment has increased, leading to a strong decline in productivity. Overall, the labour productivity of foreign firms in Tunisia decreased by 17% between 2010 and 2022, underpinned by their stalling productivity levels in manufacturing and decline in services' ICT. Policies in place, including incentives provided to export manufacturers by the offshore regime and foreign ownership restrictions in services, may have influenced the motives and composition of FDI and its mixed impact on productivity. Misreporting by firms of their revenues, labour informality and the partial reliability of existing data may also affect these results.

Beyond supporting productivity enhancements in many sectors of the economy, FDI in Tunisia also contributes to advancing innovation. Despite low levels of investment in R&D, technology diffusion from foreign firms contributes to improved innovation outcomes. Foreign firms are more R&D intensive than their Tunisian counterparts – 20% of foreign firms invested in R&D as opposed to 6% of Tunisian firms in 2021. Foreign firms are also more likely to introduce a product or process innovation, yet they tend to be less innovative than in other comparator countries, partly as a result of their specialisation in less capital-intensive activities. The share of greenfield FDI going into R&D activities is smaller than in peer economies such as Portugal, Costa Rica or Lithuania. Little FDI goes directly to R&D activities, except in the ICT and the mechanical and electronical sectors, which may help these sectors upgrade their production and export higher value-added goods and services and, in turn, improve their productivity. Sectors that are more R&D intensive, like biotechnology, medical devices or engines and turbines, do not attract much FDI in Tunisia.

Policy directions

- **Align investment policy and promotion goals with Tunisia Vision 2035** and national plans aiming at making Tunisia a knowledge-based economy with human capital as a source of innovation. This implies further promotion efforts to attract FDI in the digital economy and high-productivity services such as ICT, business services, and scientific activities. In manufacturing, supporting expansions in higher value-added activities of the automotive and electronics sectors can boost export sophistication, productivity, and knowledge spillovers, and could be more cost-effective than attracting new investors motivated by incentives of the offshore regime.
- **Improve efforts to promote local supplier network to strengthen linkages between foreign and Tunisian firms**, particularly between foreign offshore and domestic onshore companies to reduce reliance on imports of intermediate goods and services. This requires reducing administrative barriers and improving co-ordination across the investment, innovation and SME development policy and related institutions, including FIPA Tunisia, APII, and TIA.
- **Continue efforts reducing the dichotomy between the offshore and onshore regimes to** expand investors' motives beyond low value-added, export-processing, investments to more productive segments of the value chain. This includes reducing tax and regulatory differences, beyond corporate income tax, between the two regimes and stepping-up efforts to promote FDI outside of the offshore regime while improving the onshore regime attractiveness, including by removing barriers such as the requirement for foreign investors to partner with Tunisian firms.
- **Strengthen pro-competition reforms to unleash economy-wide productivity gains** following the National Strategy for Improving the Business Climate. Consider reassessing regulatory restrictions to foreign investment, notably horizontal restrictions and those in service sectors, such as business services, ICT, and transport, and, where relevant, streamline or remove them. Services restrictions can hold back economy-wide productivity gains, including in manufacturing activities relying on competitive and quality services.
- **Establish robust monitoring and evaluation mechanisms to effectively assess the impact of FDI on productivity, innovation, and GVC integration.** This requires availability and access to firm-level statistics, building on the Répertoire National des Enterprises (RNE), providing information on foreign ownership, value-added, export, and R&D spending. This will necessitate improving institutional coordination between the INS, FIPA Tunisia, and the INS.

2.2. Productivity trends and challenges in Tunisia

Private investment in Tunisia and past economic policies have contributed to the development of a well-diversified, export-oriented economy with strong manufacturing and services sectors and an important agricultural activity. Trade intensity – the share of exports and imports in GDP – reached 111% in 2022, twice as high as the OECD average. Despite a sustained pace of reforms and a diversified economy that is well integrated in international trade, private investment has dropped and productivity has stalled since 2011 (Zribi, Dhaoui and Faydi, 2016[1]). Competition and private investment are hindered by a number of long-standing barriers such as an overprotective regulatory environment, bureaucratic burdens, corruption, and difficulties to access credit (ITCEQ, 2023[2]; OECD, 2022[3]). Moreover, the repeated government changes since 2011 have brought political uncertainty that undermined business confidence.

2.2.1. *Tunisia's labour productivity growth has stalled in the past decade*

In 2022, investment accounted for 16% of GDP, well below comparators, declining from 25% in 2000. Economic growth slowed after 2011 and real GDP per worker – a measure of labour productivity – was around 40% of the OECD average in 2022 (Figure 2.1, panel A). The economy continues to exhibit a level of labour productivity that is comparable to or higher than that of other emerging economies, such as Colombia, Morocco, and Thailand. Labour productivity increased steadily at an average growth rate of 2.2% between 1991 and 2010 but has since fallen below 1%. Declining productivity growth is not specific to Tunisia, yet the pace of slowdown has left the economy behind peer countries and is inhibiting strong and inclusive growth that raises human capital, generates better incomes and helps Tunisia meet the SDGs (Figure 2.1, panel B).

Figure 2.1. Productivity trends and cross-country comparison

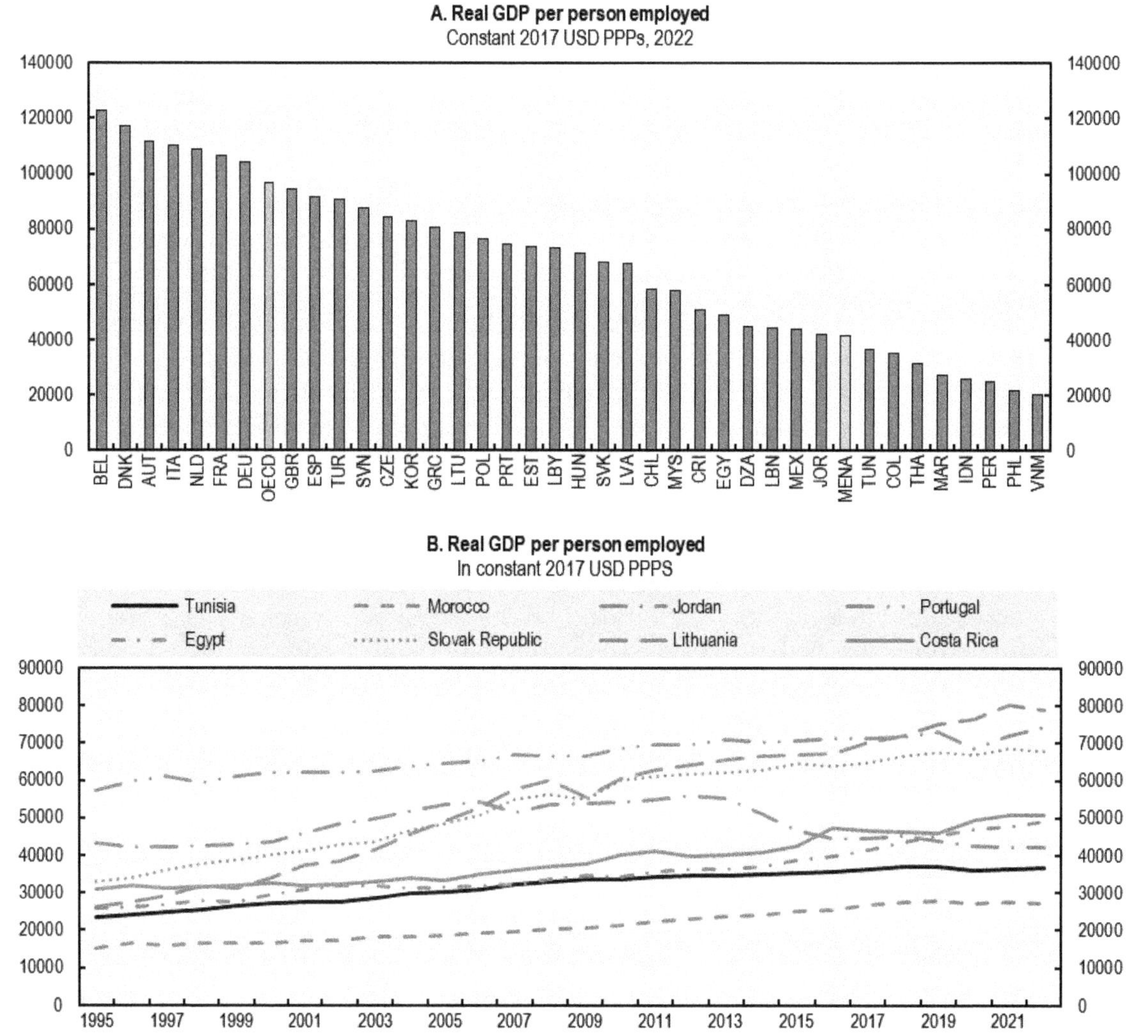

Source: World Bank Development Indicators (World Bank, 2024[4]), https://databank.worldbank.org/source/world-development-indicators.

Stalling labour productivity in Tunisia is driven by a limited productivity growth within sectors but also a slow reallocation of resources – capital and labour – to more productive sectors due to barriers to firm entry and exit, hindering business dynamism and discouraging the creation of better jobs (Amara, Zidi and Jeddi, 2022[5]; OECD, 2022[3]). Real labour productivity – measured as value added per worker – has been stagnant or even declined across sectors in the past decade. Finance and mining are the most productive sectors, which is expected as both are capital-intensive, but labour productivity of the mining sector halved between 2011 and 2020 due to disruptions in phosphates production, and growth has been almost flat for the financial sector (Figure 2.2). Labour productivity in manufacturing corresponds to around 60% of that in services, reflecting specialisation in low value-added manufacturing. Productivity in important manufacturing sectors, such as textiles and leather and mechanicals and electronics, is declining since 2011. The textiles and clothing sector used to be Tunisia's primary export industry but has faced increasing international competition in recent years, particularly from Southeast Asian countries (Ministère de l'Industrie, des Mines et de l'Énergie, 2022[6]). The productivity of the mechanical and electronics sector has declined in the past decade, falling below the national average. Resource reallocation to high-productivity sectors such as ICT is limited.

Larger and younger firms are more productive in Tunisia (Amara, Zidi and Jeddi, 2022[5]). However, business dynamism and new firm entry has been low, and an overwhelming majority of firms are micro or small enterprises, thus limiting their contribution to overall productivity growth. The significant state involvement in the economy also hinders productivity. Many sectors are dominated by large state-owned enterprises (SOEs) or private firms that enjoy monopoly power and market protection, limiting the entrance of new, younger firms. The SOE share in turnover of the largest 100 firms in Tunisia exceeds 50%, against an OECD average of 13%, and their sales amount to almost 10% of GDP (OECD, 2022[3]).

Figure 2.2. The evolution of labour productivity in Tunisia

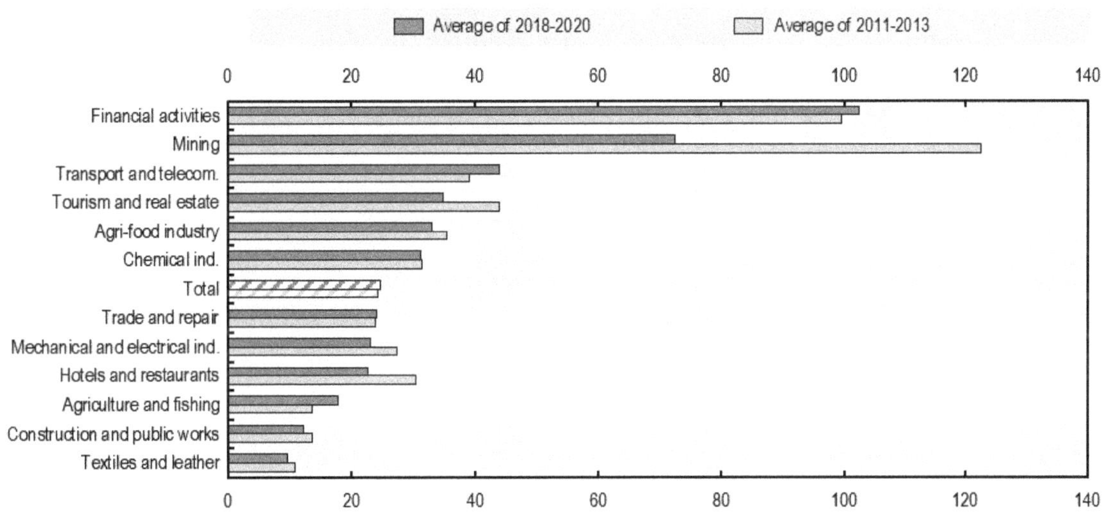

Note: Labour productivity is measured as value added per worker.
Source: OECD calculations based on (INS, 2023[7]), https://ins.tn/statistiques/75.

2.2.2. *Most of the economic activity is concentrated in low-value added sectors*

The dominance of sectors with low value-added activities in Tunisia contributes to limited labour productivity growth. Within the manufacturing sector, mechanics and electronics, food and beverages, and textiles and leather form the basis of Tunisian industry, representing 71% of all value added in the manufacturing sector in 2022 (Figure 2.3, panel A). This contribution is closely linked to the export structure of Tunisian goods, which have been an important driver of economic growth, as almost half of all manufacturing production is export-oriented (Ministère de l'Industrie, des Mines et de l'Énergie, 2022[6]). The mechanics and electronics sector represented 42% of exported goods in 2022 and is now the principal driver of Tunisia's exports, consisting mainly of electrical wires and cables produced for the European automobile industry. The other two main manufacturing sectors, the textile and leather sector and the agrifood industry, contributed to 19% and 12% of all goods exports respectively. Many exported goods are simply assembled in Tunisia, from imported intermediate parts, thus limiting the value added in these sectors (World Bank, 2014[8]). Although, over recent years, mid- and high-tech manufacturing exports within the mechanical and electrical sector have increased.

Among services, the retail and repair sector, public administration, and education were key contributors to value added, followed by transport, health and social services, and financial services (Figure 2.3, panel B). The high share of trade and repair sectors in total value-added results from the large number of companies operating in these sectors rather than their value creating potential. These sectors account for 42% of all private sector firms in Tunisia but are dominated by micro enterprises with limited growth and investment potential as well as high levels of informal employment, all of which hamper productivity growth (Dhaoui, 2022[9]). Overall, the significant growth in services is mostly due to the expansion of public administration, and less to the dynamism of high value-added tertiary activities (OECD, 2022[3]).

Figure 2.3. Economic structure of Tunisia and comparable countries

Share of value added by sector, 2022 (%)

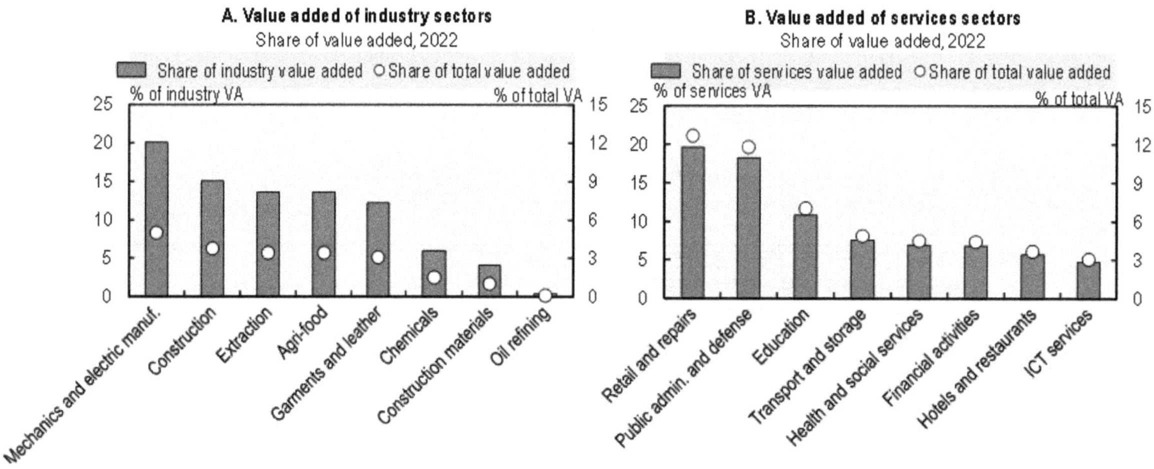

Source: OECD based on (INS, 2023[7]), https://ins.tn/statistiques/75.

2.3. The contribution of FDI to labour productivity

Foreign investment can help unlock potential productivity gains in Tunisia and boost economic growth. Foreign firms are typically more efficient, technology- and skills-intensive than average in host countries, and thus direct contributors to productivity growth. Their operations can also indirectly boost productivity among domestic firms (OECD, 2022[10]; OECD, 2023[11]). Domestic firms that supply foreign entrants see productivity gains through their improved access to knowledge, technology and finance. Other firms benefit from imitating more productive peers or by hiring workers that have gained new skills through their work with foreign firms. Benefits do not materialise automatically, however, and policies and institutional factors play an important role in enabling FDI spillovers. Realising this potential in Tunisia depends in large part on the establishment of linkages between foreign multinationals and domestic SMEs. The type, motives, and sector of the investment, as well as the size, structure and technological advantages of the investing firm all affect the extent to which Tunisia benefits from productivity spillovers.

2.3.1. Foreign investment in more productive sectors is significant

A significant share of FDI in Tunisia is in the relatively more productive sectors, with a gradual shift towards more technology- and skill-intensive sectors (Dhaoui, 2022[9]). The most productive financial sector was the second highest in terms of FDI inflows. Moreover, one fourth of FDI over 2013-2022 flowed to the four most productive sectors, excluding energy: finance; tourism and real estate; chemicals; and food and beverages (Figure 2.4, panel A). The largest share of FDI went to the mechanical and electrical sector, which also includes the metal industry. This broad sector had a limited contribution to overall productivity growth, but this may mask productivity differences within different sub-sectors. Some relatively productive sectors, such as food and beverages, have stricter restrictions on foreign ownership, potentially limiting the contribution of FDI in these sectors.

While a significant share of FDI goes to more productive industries, there is evidence of an inverse relationship between labour productivity and the number of FDI projects in Tunisia. Sectors that are more productive had a smaller share in total FDI projects during 2013-2022 and vice versa. A significant number of FDI projects is therefore concentrated in low value-added activities with modest levels of labour productivity. For example, the textile and leather sector accounted for around 5% of FDI inflows but almost 20% of all FDI projects (Figure 2.4, panel B). There is therefore a lot of FDI activity happening in this sector but since it is less capital-intense in nature, it contributed little to overall productivity levels. On the other hand, the financial, tourism and real estate sectors accounted together for around 10% of total FDI but just 2% of FDI projects, confirming the very capital-intensive nature of FDI in these sectors.

Figure 2.4. The relationship between FDI and labour productivity across sectors

Aggregate for 2013-2022

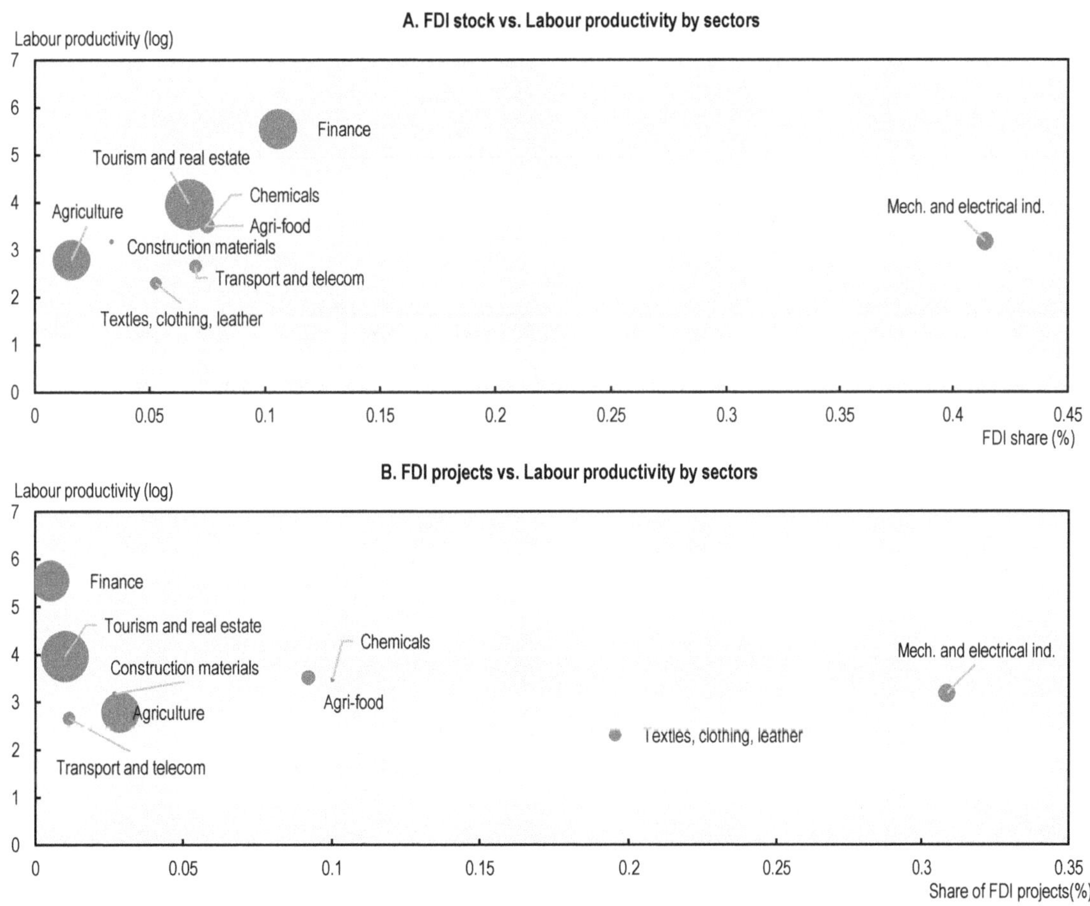

Note: The size of the bubble represents the share of a sector in total value added. FDI share by sector excludes the energy sector. The period of analysis is limited by data availability.
Source: OECD calculations based on (FIPA, 2023[12]) and (INS, 2023[7]).

2.3.2. Foreign firms are more productive than Tunisian firms in most sectors but not in those where they are largely present

Despite a significant share of FDI in productive sectors of the economy, there is scope to further improve the contribution of foreign firms to labour productivity through their direct operations. Tunisia's National Business Registry, the *RNE*, shows that foreign firms were 43% less productive than Tunisian firms in 2022, a significant drop from 2010 when both had similar productivity levels (Figure 2.5) (Box 2.1 provides more details on the data and its limitations). Overall, between 2010 and 2022, foreign firms' labour productivity decreased by 17% while that of Tunisian firms increased by 30%. The manufacturing sector, due to its greater size, is largely responsible for the negative labour productivity premium of foreign firms.

Figure 2.5. Foreign firms' total labour productivity performance has been weak and declining

Foreign labour productivity premium (a value higher than zero indicates a better performance of foreign firms)

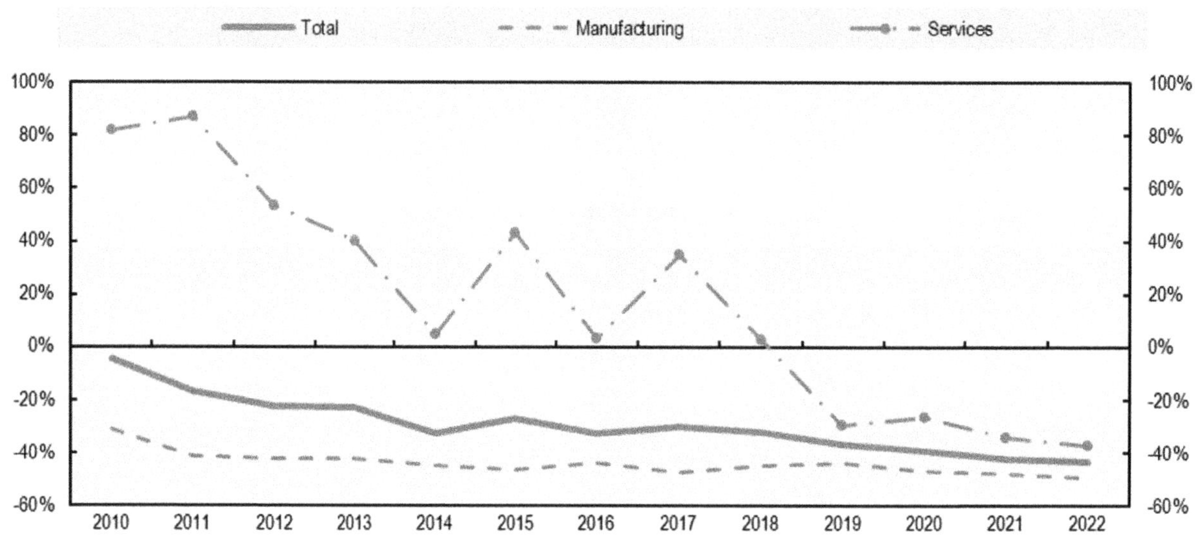

Note: Labour productivity is measured as revenues per employee. Real values were obtained by deflating by the consumer price index. The figure excludes agriculture, construction and the trade sectors where informal employment is prevalent.
Source: OECD calculations based on (INS, 2023[13]), the Répertoire National des Entreprises (RNE) sample.

Box 2.1. The National Business Registry – Répertoire National des Entreprises

Overview of the registry

The National Business Registry, *Répertoire National des Entreprises* (RNE), managed by the National Statistics Office of Tunisia (INS), provides an exhaustive list of private sector companies in Tunisia. The database is based on compiled files from the tax authorities (Direction Générale des Impôts - DGI) for company information and the national social security fund (Caisse Nationale de Securité Sociale - CNSS) for information on employment. Summary statistics on firms and employment evolution are published annually by the INS and include information broken down by sector, firm size, location, regime of operation (offshore/onshore), and ownership (Tunisian/Foreign). Information on firms' exports, imports, revenues and payroll is not available for all firms and not published in annual reports.

The sample used in this report

The INS has provided the OECD a sample of aggregated data that includes only companies that provided information on employment, revenues and payroll in order to ensure a consistency of coverage of labour productivity and wage variables (Chapter 3). Despite a reduced number of firms relative to the original RNE database, the sample provides a good coverage as it accounts for at least 80% of employment and 70% of firms with at least one employee (see details in Annex A). Strong labour informality in agriculture, construction and retail and wholesale trade may alter aggregate measures of labour productivity. In the agriculture sector, over 80% of workers are employed informally while the share in construction and the trade sectors is around 70% and 65% respectively (INS, 2020[14]). It is likely that employment numbers in these sectors are highly underestimated. Therefore, these sectors were excluded from calculations of total labour productivity and wages of foreign and Tunisian firms.

Caveats of the analysis

- *Selection bias*: As the data on turnover and wage bill is not compulsory for firms to report, there might be a selection bias as to which firms are included in the RNE sample.
- *Informal employment*: In Tunisia, informality is widespread across the economy, estimated at 45% of total economy in 2019. Employment data is therefore likely to be underestimated.
- *The definition of foreign firm*: There is no harmonised definition of foreign firms in the RNE. Firms can be defined as foreign as long as there is foreign participation in the ownership of the company.
- *Use of revenues for labour productivity measurement*: The use of revenues in labour productivity measurement is less reliable than using value added since revenues do not account for the cost of inputs used by the firm in production. Nevertheless, revenues have been commonly used to calculate productivity in the absence of value added measures.

Source: INS, Répertoire National des Entreprises.

Stalling labour productivity levels in manufacturing, combined with a strong decline in services sectors have underpinned the relatively low and deteriorating productivity performance of foreign firms in Tunisia (Figure 2.6, Panels A and B). Productivity differences between foreign and Tunisian firms are higher in manufacturing than services, but in manufacturing the gap has been constant over the past decade, whereas it increased in services in the past years. The disparity between foreign and Tunisian firms' productivity levels partly reflects the labour-intensive nature of FDI – foreign firms have a significantly higher share in total employment than in revenues compared with Tunisian firms (Table 2.1).

Figure 2.6. Foreign firms' labour productivity performance in manufacturing and services

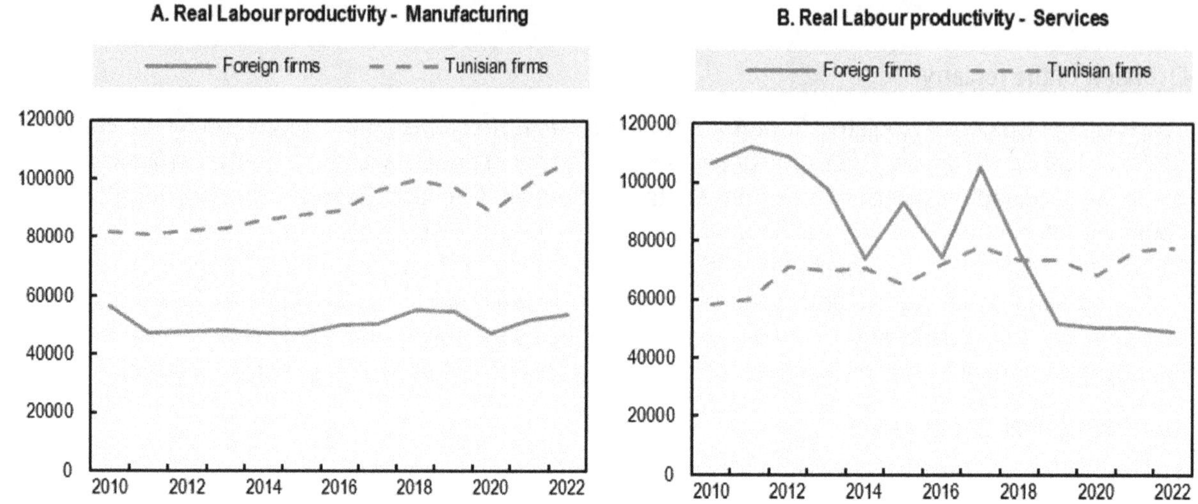

Note: Labour productivity is measured as revenues per employee. Real values were obtained by deflating by the consumer price index.
Source: OECD calculations based on (INS, 2023[13]), the Répertoire National des Entreprises (RNE) sample.

Table 2.1. Foreign firms have a higher share in total employment than in revenues

2010-2022 average

	Share of foreign companies in revenues	Share of foreign companies in employment
Total	12.6	20.2
Manufacturing	20.5	31.6
Services	7.8	9.8

Source: OECD calculations based on (INS, 2023[13]), the Répertoire National des Entreprises (RNE) sample.

Despite the negative foreign productivity premium at the national level, foreign firms are more productive than their Tunisian peers within most sectors, including important sectors such as chemicals, finance, mining, scientific and technical activities, and textiles (Figure 2.7, panel B). The few sectors where foreign firms are less productive account for 45% of foreign firms' revenues, however, and are dominated by automotive and electric-electronics manufacturers, which, combined, represent almost one third of all the foreign firms' revenues, as well as ICT services providers (Box 2.2). The discrepancy between foreign productivity premia at the national and sectoral levels is similar to findings for offshore firms, where productivity premia existed at sectoral but not at the national level (Dhaoui, 2019[15]).

Figure 2.7. Foreign firms are more productive than their Tunisian peers in most sectors

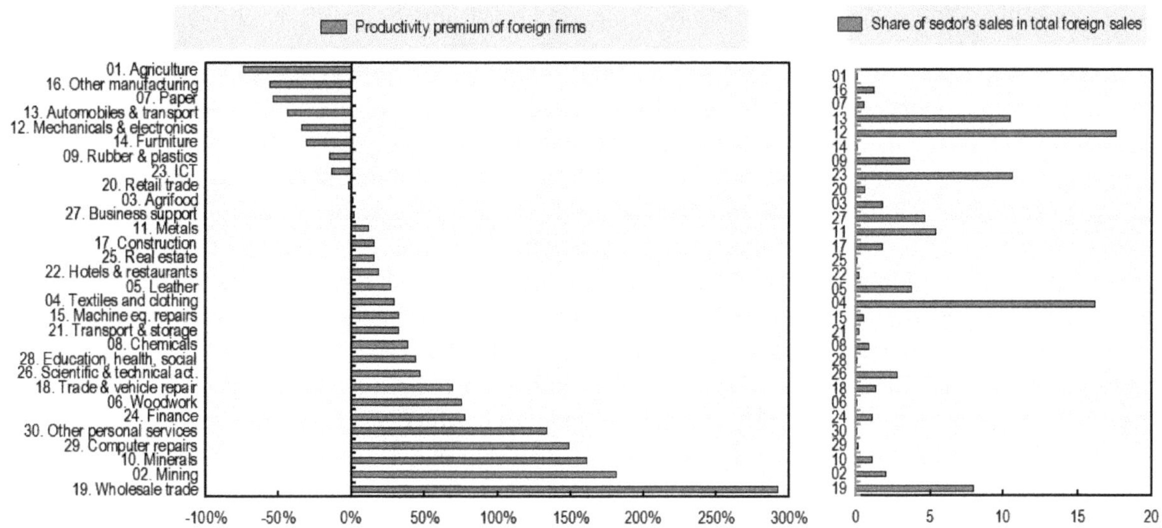

Source: OECD calculations based on (INS, 2023[13]), the Répertoire National des Entreprises (RNE) sample.

The fact that foreign firms have lower productivity in some sectors is consistent with the fact that they specialise in lower value added activities. These firms operate mainly under the offshore regime and import a large share of their inputs, which are then assembled and re-exported (Joumard, Dhaoui and Morgavi, 2018[16]). While previous studies have identified a positive link between being an offshore enterprise and productivity performance in Tunisia, the opposite holds in the case of two-way offshoring i.e. when firms export and import at the same time (Baghdadi, Kheder and Arouri, 2019[17]). Instead, these firms might be motivated to shift offshore to decrease the fixed costs associated with exporting and are likely to exit the market once privileges are removed. Similar results were also observed for example in China, where exporting firms that specialised in processing and benefitted from tariff exempted imported goods were less productive than non-processing exporters and non-exporters (Dai, Maitra and Yu, 2016[18]).

The low foreign labour productivity premium may also be the result of data limitations. In a few sectors, trends between employment and revenues growth are not consistent. In the ICT sector – the main services sector for foreign firms in terms of revenues, total revenues dropped sharply in 2019, while employment increased, resulting in a strong reduction in labour productivity. It is possible that some firms underreport revenues and overreport wages. A recent study on Tunisia has found that almost one in ten companies do not submit a tax declaration in spite of reporting workers to the social security administration, and 15% of those who do report taxes report anomalously low sales (Rijkers, Arouri and Baghdadi, 2017[19]). Similarly, tax evasion in Tunisia has been linked with firms' reporting higher labour costs (see Chapter 3) (Baghdadi, Kheder and Arouri, 2019[17]). The underreporting of revenues may be more widespread in the absence of financial controls and audits in companies. Financial audits are less common in Tunisia than in other countries, with only 25% of firms reporting that they had their financial statements reviewed by external auditors, in contrast to 59% in MENA economies and 46% in OECD countries (World Bank, 2024[20]).

Box 2.2. Labour productivity developments in key sectors of the Tunisian economy

Four sectors, representing around half of the total revenues of foreign firms, have shaped labour productivity developments of foreign firms between 2010 and 2022: i) mechanical-electrical-electronics manufacturing, ii) automotives and other transport equipment, iii) textiles and clothing and iv) ICT services. Except in textiles and clothing, labour productivity of foreign firms in these sectors was lower than that of Tunisian peers (Figure 2.8). In the mechanical and electronics sector, foreign labour productivity decreased significantly, and was 40% less than the productivity of Tunisian firms in 2022. In the automotive sector, the productivity of foreign firms slightly increased but less than the productivity of Tunisian firms. In textiles and clothing, foreign firms' productivity is higher than Tunisian peers but the gap narrowed following improvements among Tunisian firms. Total labour productivity of foreign firms in the ICT sector declined considerably and, since 2018, became lower than Tunisian ICT firms' productivity – In 2019, Tunisian firms in the ICT sector reported a six-fold increase in revenues while employment only doubled. Annex Figure 2.B.1 includes labour productivity development of foreign and Tunisian firms in additional sectors.

Figure 2.8. Foreign and Tunisian firms' labour productivity developments in selected sectors

Real revenues per employee, by ownership

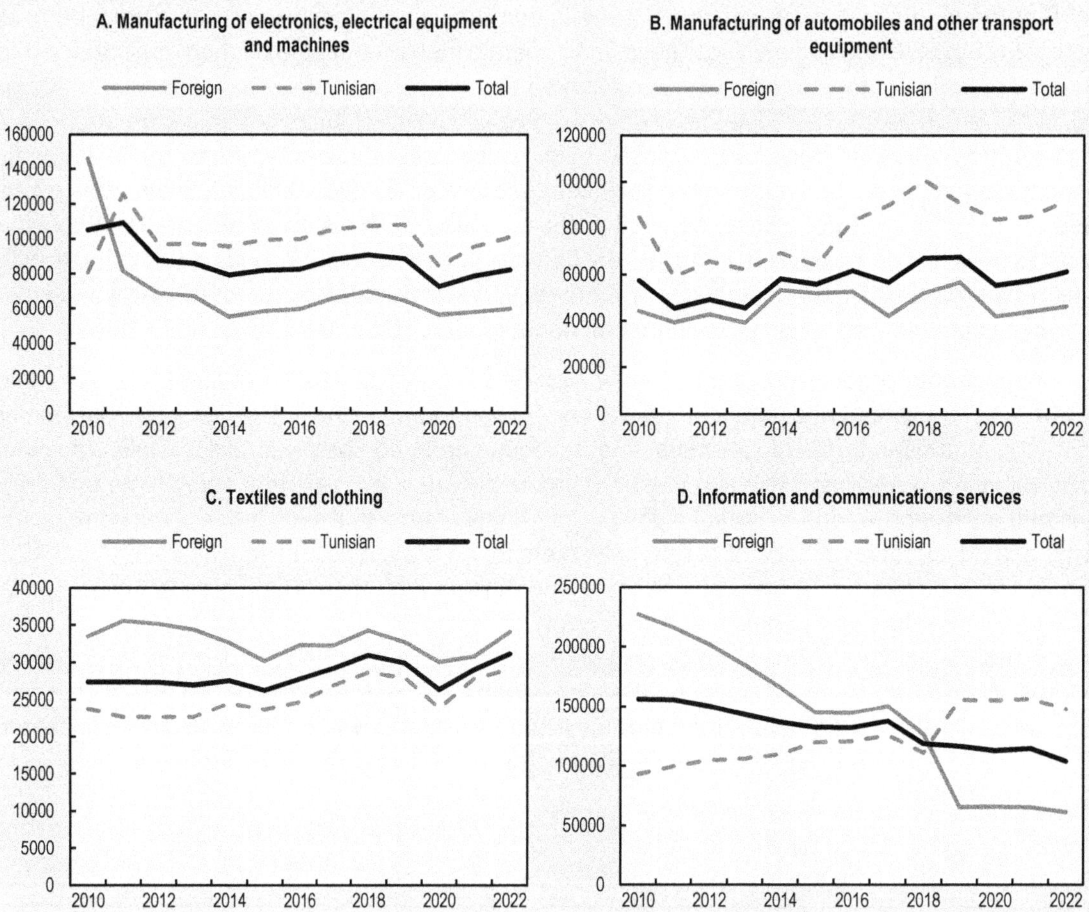

Note: Labour productivity is measured as revenues per employee. Real values were obtained by deflating by the consumer price index.
Source: OECD calculations based on (INS, 2023[13]), the Répertoire National des Entreprises (RNE) sample.

2.3.3. Tunisia's FDI contribution to productivity is lower than in other emerging economies

Internationally comparable data, based on firm-reported surveys (World Bank Enterprise Survey – WBES), shed additional light on the performance of foreign firms in Tunisia compared to peer countries. Foreign investment contributes positively to productivity growth in Tunisia, but less than in other MENA economies. The WBES data, whose sectoral coverage differs from the RNE, shows that labour productivity of foreign firms was on average 50% higher than that of domestic firms (Figure 2.9). The survey-based data might be less sensitive to underreporting than official tax administration data as they are not linked to potential tax advantages. Moreover, it measures labour productivity in terms of value added per worker and thus accounts for the actual value creation of a firm rather than what it sells. The average foreign productivity premium is still nevertheless slightly lower than the average in OECD countries and significantly lower than in other MENA economies such as Morocco, Jordan, and Egypt.

Figure 2.9. Productivity premium of foreign firms in Tunisia and comparator countries

Foreign firms are more productive if index >0, 2020 or latest year available

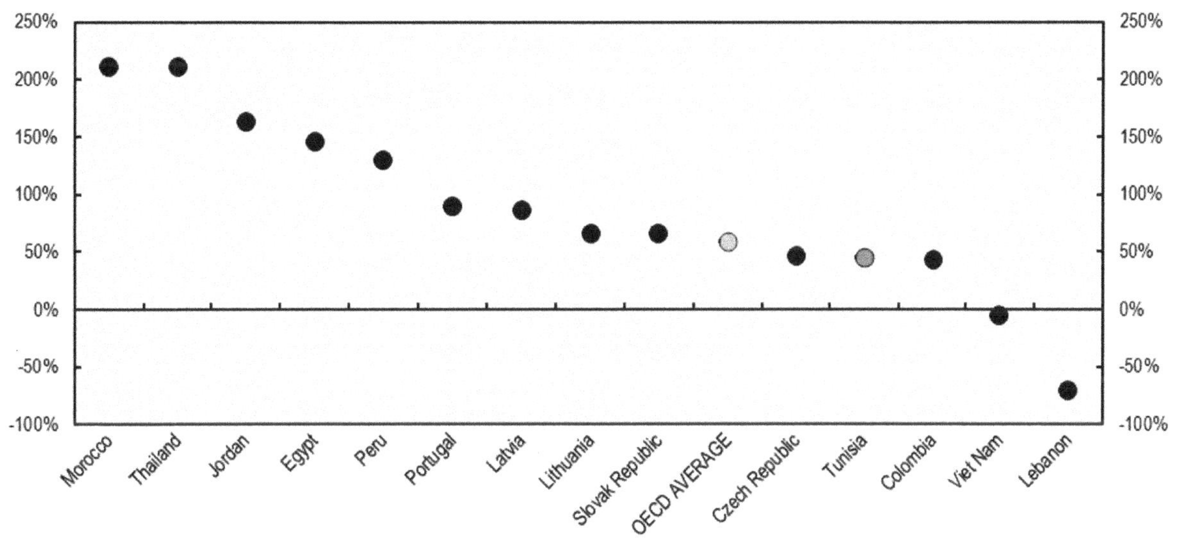

Note: Labour productivity is defined as the ratio of value added to employment.
Source: OECD calculations based on (World Bank, 2024[20]), World Bank Enterprise Surveys, https://www.enterprisesurveys.org/en/data.

2.4. The contribution of FDI to R&D and innovation

2.4.1. R&D investment and innovation outcomes in Tunisia can be improved …

As foreign firms are often larger and have more resources to engage in research and development (R&D) activities, they can contribute positively to the Tunisian economy through innovation diffusion. Technological advancements, which increase the efficiency of production or lead to product innovation, enable companies to gain a competitive edge on the market. A company can invest in R&D activities, innovate or adopt an already existing technology on the market. The more firms in Tunisia spend on R&D and innovate, the stronger will be the overall level of market competition. Moreover, technological developments at economy-wide level are important drivers of productivity growth (OECD, 2015[21]).

Investment in R&D activities in Tunisia has been low compared to the OECD average (Figure 2.10, panel A). Despite improvements since the early 2000s, 0.7% of GDP was spent on R&D in 2019 which was roughly only one fourth of the 2.7% of GDP spent in OECD countries on average. The number had been above the MENA average throughout the early 2000s but, in recent years, this spending has been on par with the MENA average, following increased R&D expenditure in other MENA countries in the past few years and lack of additional spending in Tunisia. With a high share of graduates in science, technology, engineering, and mathematics (STEM), and a booming electronics sector, Tunisia has a strong potential to attract FDI in support of innovation driven by human capital. Innovation outcomes are still relatively weak compared to peer countries, however. Tunisia applied for 15 patents per million of population in 2017-2020, versus an OECD average of 275 patents per capita. The OECD average is driven upwards by a few very innovation-driven countries such as South Korea, Japan and the United States; however, Tunisia also fared considerably worse than comparable OECD countries such as Portugal, Latvia, or Slovakia (Figure 2.10, panel B). Tunisia performs better than MENA economies where the amount of patent applications was lower.

Figure 2.10. R&D expenditure and patents applications are low

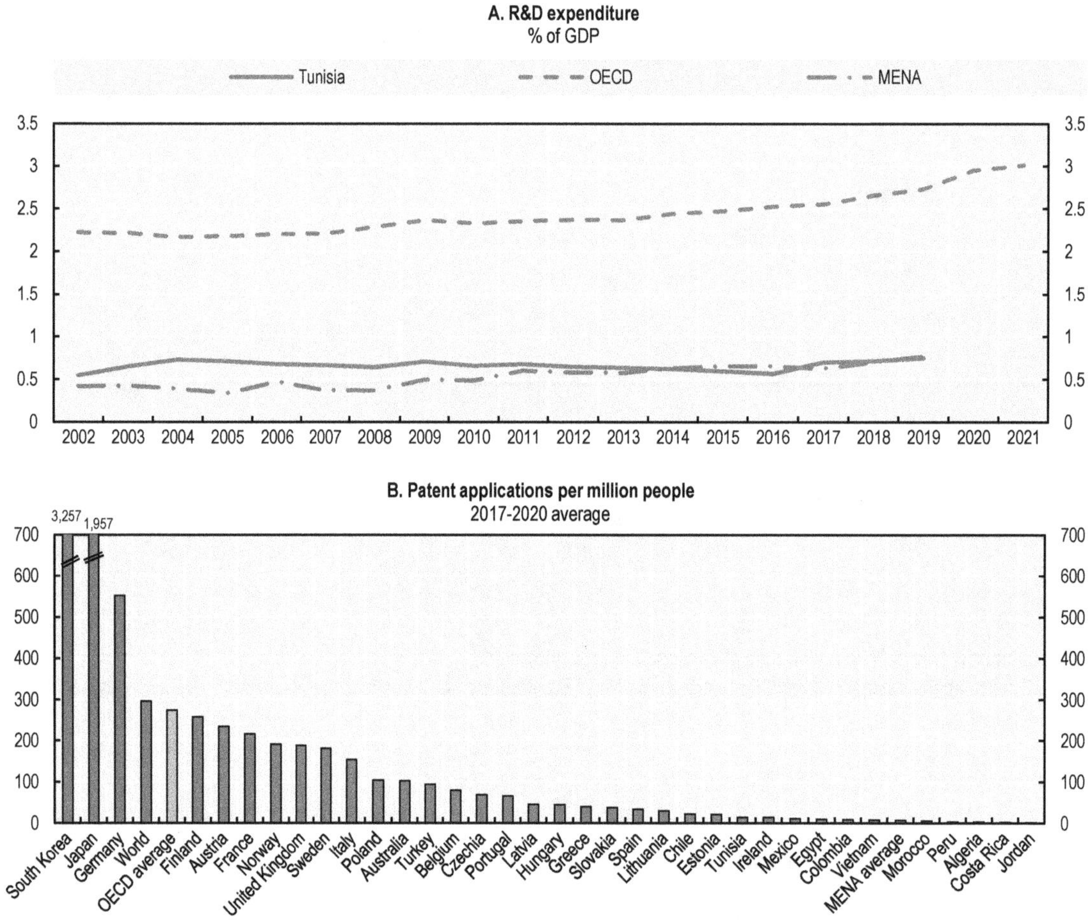

Note: In panel B, each country's data includes patent applications for which the first-named applicant is a country resident. The MENA average includes Tunisia. Egypt, Algeria, Morocco, and Jordan.
Source: World Bank Development Indicators (World Bank, 2024[4]), https://databank.worldbank.org/source/world-development-indicators.

... but foreign firms perform better than domestic ones

The presence of foreign firms in Tunisia can contribute to the overall investment and intensity of research activities in the economy. In most countries, foreign firms are more likely to invest in R&D than domestic firms (Figure 2.11, panel A). This is because they are on average larger and have a better access to finance and skilled workers and are often closer to the productivity frontier. In Tunisia, most of the research takes place in public academic institutions with little collaboration and know-how transfers to the private sector (Ministère de l'Industrie, des Mines et de l'Énergie, 2022[6]). The government has placed innovation at the centre of its industrial strategy. Yet, despite a number of existing R&D incentives set up by the government, their uptake by firms has been fairly limited. Consequently, 20% of the surveyed foreign firms in Tunisia invested in R&D as opposed to only 6% of domestic ones (Figure 2.11, panel A). One of the main constraints to increased innovation investment, reported by companies, is the lack of financial resources and difficulties accessing credit (ITCEQ, 2023[2]).

Box 2.3. Chile's High-technology Investment Promotion Programme

In the early 2000s, the Chilean Economic Development Agency (CORFO) implemented the High-Technology Investment Promotion Programme to attract high-tech investments that could diversify the productive base and position the country as an export platform of technological services in the Latin America region (Agosin, 2009[22]). The programme included financial incentives, coupled with technical assistance and information provision, for adopting advanced technologies, implementing employee training programmes, and completing pre-feasibility studies; promotional campaigns and targeted investment generation activities in major tech hubs around the world; and network development initiatives to transfer international best practices from American and European markets to Chile.

The programme's design was based on the experience of other countries, in particular Ireland and Costa Rica, whose investment promotion approach involved the targeting of incentives to specific sectors, emphasis on the technological content of promoted investments, and the use of direct subsidies rather than tax exemptions. In Chile, the prioritisation of high-technology sectors was done in line with the strategic objectives identified by the National Innovation Council for Competitiveness, an inter-institutional body responsible for co-ordinating and advising the government on innovation, science and technology policy (Agosin, 2009[22]). Efforts focused on attracting firms that could contribute to the development of the clusters identified by the Council as having the greatest potential for economic growth such as ICTs, biotechnologies and new materials.

Although the programme's budget and number of staff were small by international standards, CORFO managed to leverage the expertise of various government actors and international stakeholders. A team of government agencies was created to facilitate investment promotion activities, bringing together the National Commission for Science and Technology, Fundación Chile, a non-profit foundation that supported new technological applications in a number of industries, and Chile's IPA, the Foreign Investment Committee (Nelson, 2007[23]). To ensure alignment of the programme with industry priorities, CORFO also created a transnational strategic network consisting of a business school in the United States, sectoral experts associated with successful IPAs, US-based consulting firms specialising in business services, software development and ICTs, US business associations and foreign investors established in Chile. All played an important role in the effective development of the programme.

In 2001-03, 219 companies had received technical assistance, including information and advice for the evaluation of investment opportunities and conditions in Chile. Overall, for each US dollar of public financial support provided to foreign investors, the programme had yielded USD 10 of materialised investments (Agosin, 2009[22]). Thanks to the programme, in 2007, there were 60 international technology service centres operating in the country and leading companies in the ICT, business services, and software development sectors had been established in Chile.

Source: OECD based on Agosin (2009[22]) and Nelson (2007[23]).

As a result of increased investment, foreign firms are more likely to innovate in Tunisia. The level of innovation still lags behind many OECD countries but is similar to that observed in MENA economies. Among the firms surveyed in Tunisia, 17% of foreign firms introduced a new product or service versus 11% of domestic firms (Figure 2.11, panel B). Similar outcomes are observed regarding firms that introduced a process innovation. While in Tunisia, the number is still relatively low even for foreign firms, 10% introduced a process innovation, twice as many as domestic firms (Figure 2.11, panel C). Innovation is also correlated with trade openness as firms that export are more likely to innovate than those that sell just to the domestic market, with the mechanical and electrical sector driving innovation (Ministère de l'Industrie, des Mines et de l'Énergie, 2022[6]).

Figure 2.11. Innovation outcomes of foreign firms in Tunisia and comparator countries

2020 or latest year available

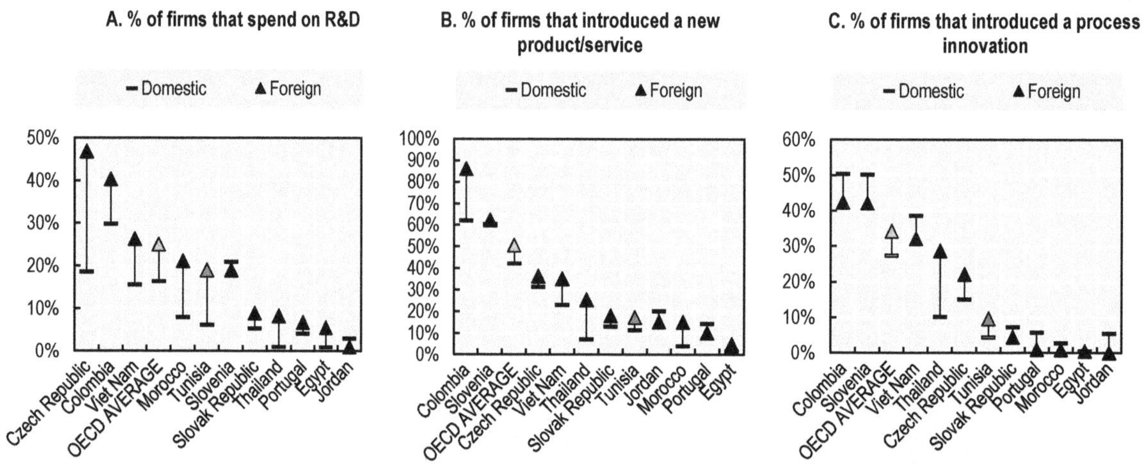

Source: OECD calculations based on (World Bank, 2024[20]), World Bank Enterprise Surveys, https://www.enterprisesurveys.org/en/data.

The fact that innovation outcomes of foreign firms in Tunisia are weak compared to other countries is related to the fact that most of them operate in relatively less capital-intensive manufacturing industries. Nevertheless, as they perform better than domestic firms on average, there is a potential for innovation diffusion to the local economy, as long as domestic firms have the absorptive capacities to adapt to new technologies or processes. Further efforts could help attract more technology-intensive FDI in Tunisia. In Chile, the government implemented the High-Technology Investment Promotion Programme to attract high-tech FDI that could diversify Chile's productive base and position the country as an export platform of technological services in Latin America (Box 2.3).

The prevalence of R&D activities in Tunisia is dependent on the sectors where firms operate as some sectors are more technology-intense than others by nature. It also depends on their position in value chains as the higher the firm is positioned in the value chain, the more important the role of innovation. Only a handful of sectors in Tunisia have greenfield FDI directed specifically at R&D, in contrast to a larger number of sectors in comparator regions (Figure 2.12, panel A). Yet, R&D investments are significant in the software and IT services sector, where the amount of FDI into R&D amounted to 55% of all the FDI in that sector over 2003-22. At the same time, the software & IT services sector is a small contributor to overall FDI and half of the R&D FDI came from a single project, therefore it does not necessarily define a trend in the sector. In the automotive sector, 14% of all FDI went towards R&D activities, and less significant amounts were present in the communications, business services, and textiles sectors. At the same time, the sectors that are relatively R&D intensive, like biotechnology, medical devices or engines and turbines, do not attract much FDI in general in Tunisia.

The share of FDI directed at R&D activities is higher than most MENA economies but falls behind some peer OECD countries like Portugal, Costa Rica or Lithuania (Figure 2.12, panel B). There is scope to diversify further the activities within sectors and attract more FDI aimed at R&D activities within the manufacturing sectors, such as in the automotive or the mechanical and electronics sectors. In the Slovak Republic, where foreign firms tend to concentrate in low value-added activities, the government has put in place reforms aiming at improving the collaboration on R&D and technology-based projects in key sectors, with the objective to diversify the economy beyond low value-added manufacturing (Box 2.3).

Figure 2.12. Greenfield FDI in R&D across sectors in Tunisia

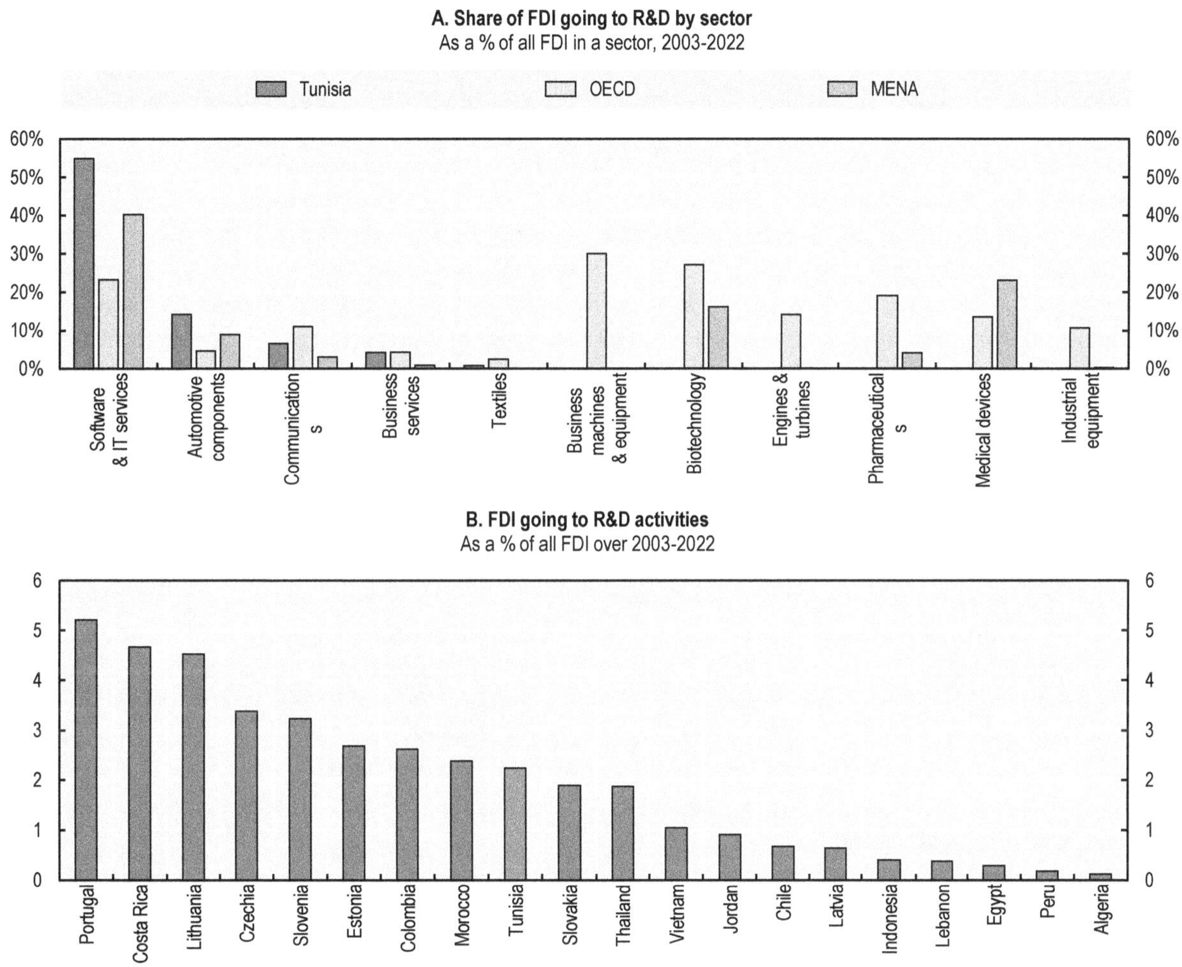

Note: Greenfield FDI corresponds to announced capital expenditure (CAPEX) and is partly based on estimates.
Source: OECD calculations based on Financial Times (2024[24]), https://www.fdimarkets.com/.

Box 2.4. FDI and economic diversification policies delivered by the Slovak IPA

The Slovak Republic shows a high level of economic specialisation. Most of its value added and employment, are concentrated in a few sectors, mainly in the automotive industry, and a number of low-tech sectors, such as wholesale and retail trade, real estate activities and construction. Although the automotive industry alone is responsible for 20% of total manufacturing value added, foreign affiliates operating in the automotive industry are involved in low value-added activities (fabrication and assembly of imported car components). Their investment generates, therefore, scarce local technology diffusion, which hampers the sector's and the overall economy's potential to upgrade to more knowledge-intensive activities.

Recent policy reforms in the Slovak Republic have focused on diversifying the economy beyond low value-added manufacturing and strengthening its innovation potential. The Regional Investment Aid Scheme is the main instrument used by the Slovak government to support investments that help the economy move away from low value-added manufacturing and towards more knowledge-intensive and high-tech sectors. The scheme provides aid in the form of grants for tangible and intangible fixed assets, corporate income tax relief, wage subsidies for newly created jobs and discounts in the renting or selling of real estate. The sectoral scope of the Regional Investment Aid Scheme illustrates the government's strategic choice to support FDI-intensive sectors to move higher up the value chain and engage in technologically sophisticated activities with more local content in their products. To benefit from the aid, investment projects should fall under one of the defined investment categories, namely industrial production, technological centres and business services centres, each one of which is linked to priority sectors (e.g. chemicals, electronics, automotive, business services etc.) and relevant smart industry technologies (e.g. robotics, artificial intelligence, big data, cloud, etc.).

In recent years, investment facilitation and aftercare services have also focused on encouraging foreign and domestic firms to collaborate on the implementation of R&D and technology-based projects. The Slovak IPA, SARIO, has established an Innovation Services Platform, which connects some of its most technologically advanced foreign clients with innovative Slovak firms to undertake R&D. In addition to policy efforts aimed at increasing the knowledge intensity of FDI (see section on productivity-enhancing FDI), similar initiatives have been recently introduced to help the Slovak SMEs diversify their activities towards high-tech sectors. In 2019, SARIO started providing diversification services to the Slovak SMEs that want to expand their operations into the space, aviation, smart mobility and medical technologies industries. The support includes business-consulting services, seminars, matchmaking events and workshops for B2B collaboration.

Source: OECD (2022[25]).

2.5. The contribution of FDI to Tunisia's integration into global value chains

Participation in GVCs allows countries to integrate into global trade, expand their presence on international markets, diversify exports and enhance domestic competition, all of which can bring positive spillovers for productivity growth and innovation. In addition, it can enhance the internationalisation of local SMEs, which are typically too small to expand beyond neighbouring countries, through establishing links with large foreign companies. The transfer of technologies and human capital can contribute to productivity spillovers on domestic firms, as long as they have the absorptive capacity to benefit from these linkages.

2.5.1. *Most foreign firms in Tunisia are fully exporting companies with weak domestic linkages*

Tunisia has become well-integrated into GVCs, following a period of trade liberalisation in the 1990s and accession to the World Trade Organisation in 1994. The government has pursued an export-led model of growth based on investment incentives, resulting in increasing flows of FDI (World Bank, 2014[8]). Trade openness has had generally positive outcomes for economic growth, increased competition and contributed to productivity improvements. The manufacturing sector has been the principal driver of exports, sustained by the mechanical and electrical as well as textiles and clothing sector. Exports are well diversified in terms of products but concentrated geographically with almost 60% of all exports going to France, Germany, and Italy, making Tunisia vulnerable to the economic situation in partner countries.

Tunisia's integration in GVCs has been partly driven by the offshore regime i.e. companies that are fully exporting and enjoying special privileges such as duty exemptions and tax privileges or advantageous access to ports. Offshore companies are not well integrated with onshore companies, limiting the spillovers from FDI (Joumard, Dhaoui and Morgavi, 2018[16]). On average, 45% of firms in the manufacturing sector which employ at least ten people are fully exporting firms (APII, 2024[26]). This number is as high as 80% in the textile and clothing sector and at around 70% in the sectors of leather and shoes, and electric and electronic manufacturing. There is also a strong link between FDI and export activity as many of the offshore firms are foreign firms. This is especially true for bigger foreign manufacturing firms, with at least 10 employees and 100% of foreign capital, where offshore firms make up 94% of all foreign firms (Table 2.2). In the two manufacturing sectors where most of these foreign firms operate i.e. the textiles and leather sector, and electric and electronic sector, 98% and 99% of companies respectively are fully exporting. In all the manufacturing sectors except the construction materials sector, offshore firms make up at least 80% of foreign companies thus limiting their interaction with the domestic market.

Table 2.2. The share of offshore companies among foreign manufacturing firms

Share and number of offshore firms among foreign and Tunisian firms, by sector

	FOREIGN FIRMS		DOMESTIC FIRMS	
	Share of offshore firms	Number of firms	Share of offshore firms	Number of firms
Agrifood industry	86%	22	17%	872
Ceramic and glass building materials industries	45%	20	2%	281
Mechanical and metallurgical industries	93%	122	11%	391
Electrical, electronic, and household appliance industries	99%	155	32%	118
Chemical industries	80%	90	10%	355
Textile and clothing industries	98%	362	71%	842
Wood, cork and furniture industries	80%	10	4%	125
Leather and shoes industry	100%	58	55%	101
Other industries	93%	40	13%	188
Total	**94%**	879	**29%**	**3273**

Note: Refers to firms with 100% of foreign or 100% Tunisian ownership. Included are only companies with at least 10 employees.
Source: Agence de Promotion de l'Industrie et de l'Innovation, (APII, 2024[26]), http://www.tunisieindustrie.nat.tn/fr/tissu.asp.

Tunisia's strong export performance and FDI attraction have helped it became well integrated into GVCs, mainly through imports of intermediate products (OECD, 2021[27]). The two main OECD GVC indicators, forward and backward participation, indicate the position of a country along the global supply chains. Forward participation shows the extent to which the value added generated in one country is integrated in another country's exports and is typically high in countries specialising in the R&D or design stages of production (OECD, 2021[27]). With a share of 16%, Tunisia's integration is lower than that of the OECD average and most of its peer countries (Figure 2.13, panel A) and reflects that the contribution of Tunisian exports in GVCs is relatively low. Despite improvements in sophistication levels of exports, only 7% of manufactured exports are of the high-technology type i.e. with high R&D intensity, in contrast with 17% on average in the OECD countries (World Bank, 2024[28]). On the other hand, Tunisia's integration through backward participation, at 35%, is higher than many comparable countries (Figure 2.13, panel B). Backward participation reflects the share of foreign value added in gross exports and suggests that many intermediate inputs for production in Tunisia are sourced from abroad, assembled and then further re-exported. This is particularly the case for exports in the mechanics and electronics, as well as textiles and leather sectors (Joumard, Dhaoui and Morgavi, 2018[16]).

Figure 2.13. Integration into GVCs across countries

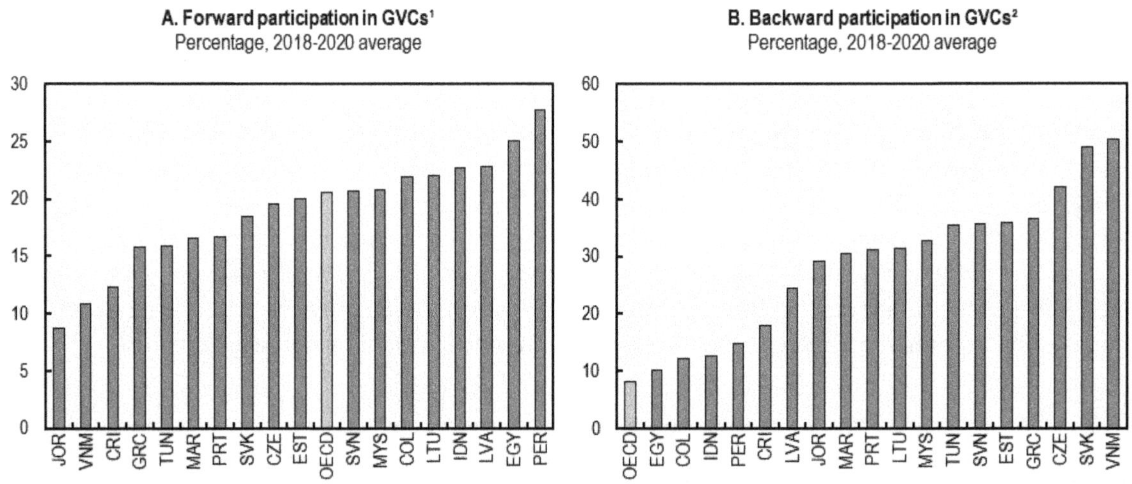

Note: 1. Domestic value added in foreign exports as a share of gross exports. 2. Foreign value added share of gross exports.
Source: OECD Trade in Value Added (TiVA) 2022 Database (OECD, 2022[29]), https://stats.oecd.org/.

2.5.2. There are positive spillovers to be gained from strengthening FDI-SME linkages

Participation in GVCs can help foster linkages between foreign and Tunisian firms. The presence of foreign firms generally encourages competition and incentivises domestic firms to innovate, with positive direct consequences on productivity. However, Tunisian firms – mostly SMEs or micro enterprises – are often financially constrained and lack skilled staff, and hence might not have adequate resources to innovate. They can nevertheless benefit from positive knowledge spillovers from FDI through labour mobility between their workers and those of foreign firms, business linkages with foreign suppliers or buyers, or through technology transfers. Establishing links between foreign and local firms allows domestic firms to participate in GVCs as foreign firms are often export-oriented multinationals serving international markets. However, the extent to which linkages between foreign and domestic firms form and positive spillovers occur would be determined by the Tunisian firms' product quality, absorptive capacities, as well as the sector it operates in. The most productive foreign firms are more demanding in terms of the quality of the product they are sourcing and local suppliers need to be able to respond to such needs (OECD, 2023[11]).

Foreign firms have limited supply linkages with Tunisian firms, partly because they mostly operate under the offshore regime, and hence benefit from tax exemptions on imported inputs while facing administrative barriers to source from Tunisian onshore firms. On average, foreign firms in Tunisia source 30% of their inputs from domestic firms, which is the lowest share among MENA economies (Figure 2.14). This reflects to some extent the large share of foreign companies in the offshore sector and the difficulties to establish links with domestic companies. Different regulations which exist between the offshore and onshore regime and the associated transaction costs, as well as low competitiveness of domestically supplied products, encourage imports of intermediates from abroad (Joumard, Dhaoui and Morgavi, 2018[16]). As a result, 46% of imported intermediates in Tunisia are re-exported.

Domestic firms purchase two-thirds of their inputs from local firms, reflecting a duality in the supply chains between domestic and foreign firms. Technology spillovers from foreign to domestic firms are also limited, with only 8% of Tunisian firms using technology licensed from a foreign company, in contrast to 23% of foreign firms (Figure 2.15). Linkages between foreign and domestic firms are still limited but there is a potential for domestic companies to benefit further from the presence of foreign firms. The provision of technological inputs by foreign to domestic firms can be an important source of productivity growth in emerging economies (Newman et al., 2015[30]). There is scope for policymakers to address the challenges that domestic companies face to access foreign technology as well as promote better integration between domestic and foreign firms in order to fully benefit from the potential of the FDI-SME linkages. Example of such enabling policies include facilitating contact with the domestic suppliers, upgrading their capabilities, or financial support, such as was done in some European countries (see Box 2.5).

Figure 2.14. Sourcing from domestic firms

% of inputs sourced domestically, 2020 or latest available

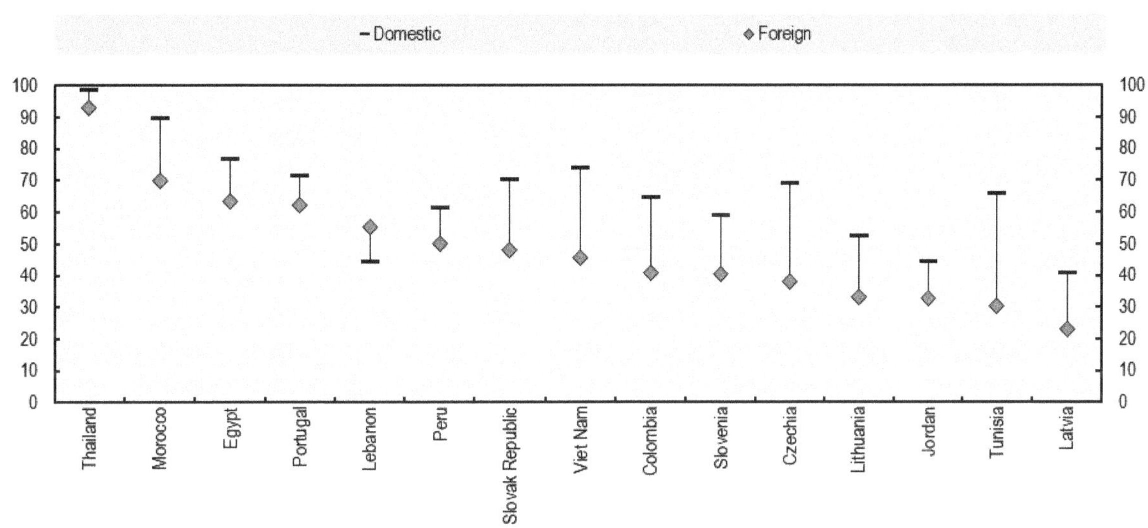

Source: OECD calculations based on World Bank Enterprise Survey, (World Bank, 2020[31]), https://www.enterprisesurveys.org/en/data.

Figure 2.15. Sourcing technology from foreign company

% of firms using technology licensed from a foreign company, 2020 or latest available

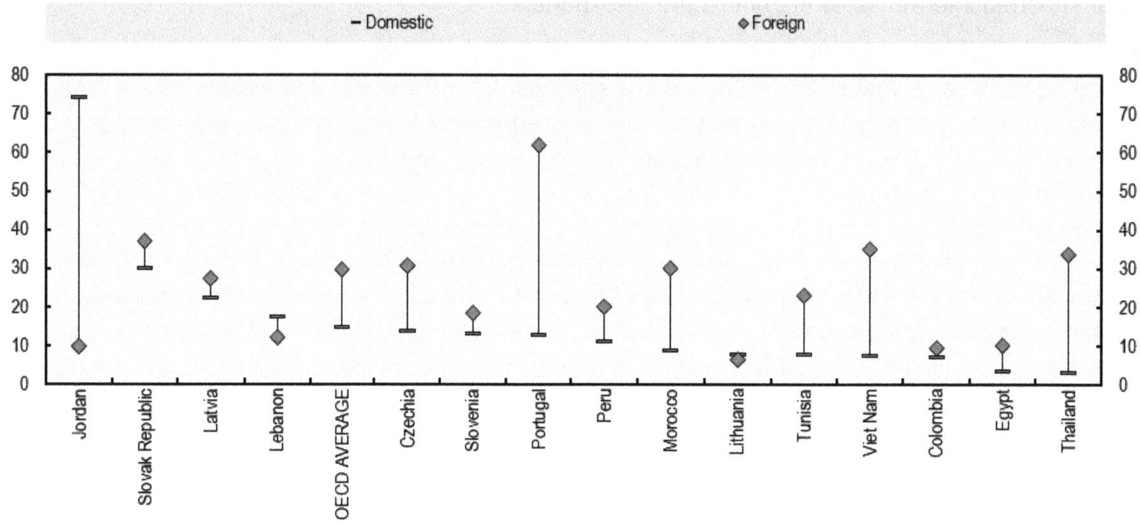

Source: OECD calculations based on World Bank Enterprise Survey, (World Bank, 2020[31]), https://www.enterprisesurveys.org/en/data.

Box 2.5 Promoting value chain linkages and strategic partnerships in selected EU countries

Matchmaking services, online platforms and events to link FDI and SMEs

Most IPAs, including Tunisia's FIPA, provide matchmaking services to reduce the information barriers that prevent foreign investors from identifying local suppliers or customers. In the Slovak Republic, SARIO supports several matchmaking programmes targeting foreign firms and their affiliates, including the flagship *Business Link* events and *Slovak Matchmaking Fairs*, implemented under the auspices of the Ministry of the Economy (OECD, 2022[25]). The use of online tools and platforms is common in this area. In Bulgaria, the national SME promotion agency BSMEPA runs an online platform to advertise requests of foreign companies looking for partners in the domestic industry (e.g. local suppliers, local exporters, potential business partners). The Hungarian Investment Promotion Agency (HIPA) maintains a database of domestic firms to help large companies identify suppliers that meet their requirements and could integrate their value chain.

Many EU governments organise or actively support the participation of domestic SMEs in knowledge exchange and information events, which can provide matching opportunities with foreign partners. The Spanish agency Red.es, in collaboration with ICEX Spain Export and Investment, organises national stands in international events to support the internationalisation of domestic firms operating in the digital economy. In Bulgaria, the BSMEPA runs a dedicated project to support domestic SMEs' participation in business fairs, exhibitions and conferences within the country and abroad, with a view to enhancing their export activities, facilitating the establishment of direct contacts and commercial linkages with foreign partners, and fostering their integration in European and international markets.

Assistance for upgrading the capabilities of domestic suppliers

Common instruments to develop value chain linkages are supplier development programmes – such as Portugal's flagship Supplier Club or the Slovak Republic' *Supply Chain Development Programme* – and other business consulting and skills upgrading schemes that seek to align the capabilities of domestic suppliers with the requirements of foreign investors. Some schemes specifically target SMEs or start-ups. In Sweden, the *Leap Accelerator* programme helps technology start-ups develop tailored go-to-market plans and build strategies for internationalisation via diverse training, consulting and peer-learning services (e.g. online collaborative workshops for groups of companies, individual coaching sessions, data-driven analysis tailored to the company's needs).

Financial support for enabling SME integration into GVCs or collaborative R&D

SMEs internationalisation through trade can facilitate market expansion and upgrading and help strengthen the domestic supplier base. The *Dutch Trade and Investment Fund (DTIF)*, set up by the Ministry of Foreign Affairs and administered by Invest International, provides loans, guarantees and export financing to domestic firms wishing to import, export or establish affiliates abroad. In Finland, Finnverra's *Internationalisation Loans* support the costs of establishing and operating SME subsidiaries abroad.

Financial support is also given for collaborative R&D and innovation activities involving foreign partners. Many of these schemes specifically target SMEs or reward their involvement with higher grant or loan rates The *German Central Innovation Programme for SMEs (ZIM)* includes two sub-schemes (ZIM cooperation projects and ZIM cooperation networks) that support with grants joint R&D&I projects by consortia of SMEs and research institutions. Since 2018, co-operative projects involving foreign partners are also eligible for funding.

Source: (OECD, 2021[32])

References

Agosin, M. (2009), "Se justifica una política industrial hacia la inversión extranjera? El Programa de Atracción de Inversiones de Alta Tecnología", *Trabajos de Investigación en Políticas Públicas, Universidad de Chile.* [22]

Amara, M., F. Zidi and H. Jeddi (2022), *Structural Change, Productivity and Job Creation: Evidence from Tunisia*, African Economic Research Consortium, http://publication.aercafricalibrary.org/handle/123456789/3431. [5]

APII (2024), *Tissu Industriel Tunisien*, http://www.tunisieindustrie.nat.tn/fr/tissu.asp. [26]

Baghdadi, L., S. Kheder and H. Arouri (2019), "Assessing the Performance of Offshore Firms in Tunisia", *Source: Journal of Economic Integration*, Vol. 34/2, pp. 280-307, https://doi.org/10.2307/26640595. [17]

Dai, M., M. Maitra and M. Yu (2016), "Unexceptional exporter performance in China? The role of processing trade", *Journal of Development Economics*, Vol. 121, pp. 177-189, https://doi.org/10.1016/j.jdeveco.2016.03.007. [18]

Dhaoui, S. (2022), *Pour un renouveau de la politique industrielle en Tunisie*, ITCEQ, http://www.itceq.tn/files/investissement-et-croissance/renouveau-de-la-politique-industrielle.pdf. [9]

Dhaoui, S. (2019), "Offshore et productivité : Analyse économétrique à partir des données de l'enquête d'entreprises de la Banque Mondiale". [15]

Financial Times (2024), *fDi Markets database*, https://www.fdimarkets.com. [24]

FIPA (2023), *Rapports annuels des IDE.* [12]

INS (2023), *Répertoire National des Entreprises (RNE) database.* [13]

INS (2023), *Valeurs ajoutées par secteur d'activité*, https://ins.tn/statistiques/75. [7]

INS (2020), *Indicateurs sur l'emploi informel 2019*, https://ins.tn/publication/indicateurs-sur-lemploi-informel-2019 (accessed on 26 January 2024). [14]

ITCEQ (2023), *Résultats de la 22eme enquete et positionnement de la Tunisie dans les rapports internationaux*, http://www.itceq.tn/files/climat-des-affaires-competitivite/2023/rapport-resultats-enquete-2022.pdf. [2]

Joumard, I., S. Dhaoui and H. Morgavi (2018), "Insertion de la Tunisie dans les chaines de valeur mondiales et role des entreprises offshore", *Documents de travail du Département des Affaires économiques de l'OCDE*, No. 1478, Éditions OCDE, Paris, https://doi.org/10.1787/546dbd75-fr. [16]

Ministère de l'Industrie, des Mines et de l'Énergie (2022), *Stratégie Industrielle et d'Innovation 2035*, http://www.tunisieindustrie.gov.tn/si2035/Livrable_7_Rapport_final.pdf. [6]

Nelson, R. (2007), "Transnational Strategic Networks and Policymaking in Chile: CORFO's High Technology Investment Promotion Program", *Latin American Politics and Society*, Vol. 49/2, pp. 149-181, https://doi.org/10.1111/j.1548-2456.2007.tb00410.x. [23]

Newman, C. et al. (2015), "Technology transfers, foreign investment and productivity spillovers", *European Economic Review*, Vol. 76, pp. 168-187, https://doi.org/10.1016/j.euroecorev.2015.02.005. [30]

OECD (2023), *Policy Toolkit for Strengthening FDI and SME Linkages*, OECD Publishing, Paris, https://doi.org/10.1787/688bde9a-en. [11]

OECD (2022), *FDI Qualities Policy Toolkit*, OECD Publishing, Paris, https://doi.org/10.1787/7ba74100-en. [10]

OECD (2022), *OECD Economic Surveys: Tunisia 2022*, OECD Publishing, Paris, https://doi.org/10.1787/7f9459cf-en. [3]

OECD (2022), *Strengthening FDI and SME Linkages in the Slovak Republic*, OECD Publishing, Paris, https://doi.org/10.1787/972046f5-en. [25]

OECD (2022), *Trade in Value Added (TiVA) Database*, https://stats.oecd.org/. [29]

OECD (2021), *EC/OECD Survey of Institutions and Policies enabling FDI-SME Linkages*, http://www.oecd.org/industry/smes/fdi-sme.htm. [32]

OECD (2021), *Middle East and North Africa Investment Policy Perspectives*, OECD Publishing, Paris, https://doi.org/10.1787/6d84ee94-en. [27]

OECD (2015), *The Future of Productivity*, OECD Publishing, Paris, https://doi.org/10.1787/9789264248533-en. [21]

Rijkers, B., H. Arouri and L. Baghdadi (2017), "Are Politically Connected Firms More Likely to Evade Taxes? Evidence from Tunisia", *Supplement: PAPERS AND PROCEEDINGS OF THE ANNUAL BANK CONFERENCE ON DEVELOPMENT ECONOMICS*, Vol. 30, pp. 166-175, https://doi.org/10.1093/wber/lhw018. [19]

World Bank (2024), *High-technology exports (indicator)*. [28]

World Bank (2024), *World Bank Development Indicators database*, https://databank.worldbank.org/source/world-development-indicators. [4]

World Bank (2024), *World Bank Enterprise Surveys*, https://www.enterprisesurveys.org/en/data. [20]

World Bank (2020), *World Bank Enterprise Survey: Tunisia*. [31]

World Bank (2014), *The Unfinished Revolution: Bringing Opportunity, Good Jobs And Greater Wealth To All Tunisians*, World Bank Group, Washington D.C., https://documents.worldbank.org/en/publication/documents-reports/documentdetail/658461468312323813/the-unfinished-revolution-bringing-opportunity-good-jobs-and-greater-wealth-to-all-tunisians. [8]

Zribi, Y., S. Dhaoui and N. Faydi (2016), *Investissement privé en Tunisie: bilan et perspectives*, ITCEQ, http://www.itceq.tn/files/investissement-et-croissance/investissement-prive.pdf. [1]

Annex 2.A. Comparison of the RNE sample with the original registry

The table below compares the number of firms and employees by sector in the original RNE database and the sample provided by INS to the OECD. Included are only firms with at least one employee.

Annex Table 2.A.1. Comparison of the RNE sample with the original registry by sector

2021

Sector name	Number of firms in RNE	Number of firms in Sample	***Share of firms covered in the sample***	Number of employees in RNE	Number of Workers in the sample	***Share of workers covered in the sample***
Agriculture and fishing	1332	796	***59.8***	23392.58	19653.5	***84.0***
Mining	424	266	***62.7***	7383.41	4600.4166	***62.3***
Agrifood manufacturing	5595	3792	***67.8***	69303.5	61514.917	***88.8***
Manufacture of textiles and clothing	3354	2466	***73.5***	161938.75	141980.75	***87.7***
Manufacture of leather and shoes	544	373	***68.6***	23656.91	21167.5833	***89.5***
Manufacture of paper and paper products; printing and reproduction	769	602	***78.3***	13931.92	12931.083	***92.8***
Manufacture of chemicals and pharmaceuticals	789	613	***77.7***	20321	19282.5833	***94.9***
Manufacture of rubber and plastics products	674	536	***79.5***	22013.42	19700.584	***89.5***
Manufacture of other non-metallic mineral products	806	567	***70.3***	23635.08	21201.25	***89.7***
Manufacture of basic metals and fabricated metal products, except machinery and equipment	2293	1705	***74.4***	27874.25	24555.333	***88.1***
Manufacture of computer, electronic and optical products; Manufacture of electrical equipment; Manufacture of machinery and equipment n.e.c.	975	800	***82.1***	98896.75	96742.5	***97.8***
Manufacture of motor vehicles, trailers and semi-trailers, and other transport equipment	261	201	***77.0***	45449.75	42882.084	***94.4***
Repair and installation of machinery and equipment	676	484	***71.6***	5176.25	3975.7501	***76.8***
Other manufacturing	2632	1854	***70.4***	7577.08	7160.9167	***94.5***
Construction	6543	4248	***64.9***	46206.59	38202.3337	***82.7***
Wholesale and retail trade and repair of motor vehicles and motorcycles	3666	2786	***76.0***	16261.92	13197.75	***81.2***
Wholesale trade, except of motor vehicles and motorcycles	10138	7800	***76.9***	65473.5	57866.417	***88.4***
Retail trade, except of motor vehicles and motorcycles	14263	11183	***78.4***	65576.33	57290	***87.4***

Transport and storage	3387	2008	***59.3***	30441	23960.667	***78.7***
Accommodation and food service activities	8458	5396	***63.8***	47636.58	35790.167	***75.1***
Information and communication	2746	1953	***71.1***	33774.75	28634	***84.8***
Financial and insurance activities	967	742	***76.7***	24798.17	24180.333	***97.5***
Professional, scientific and technical activities	8165	6023	***73.8***	35230.75	27646.9164	***78.5***
Administrative and support service activities	3250	2171	***66.8***	95385.25	70955.5	***74.4***
Education; Health and social work	12657	9885	***78.1***	49497.5	40611.417	***82.0***

Note: Included are only firms with at least one employee.
Source: (INS, 2023[13]), Répertoire National des Entreprises.

Annex 2.B. Labour productivity developments of foreign and Tunisian firms across sectors

Annex Figure 2.B.1. Foreign and Tunisian firms' labour productivity developments in selected sectors

Real revenues per employee, by ownership

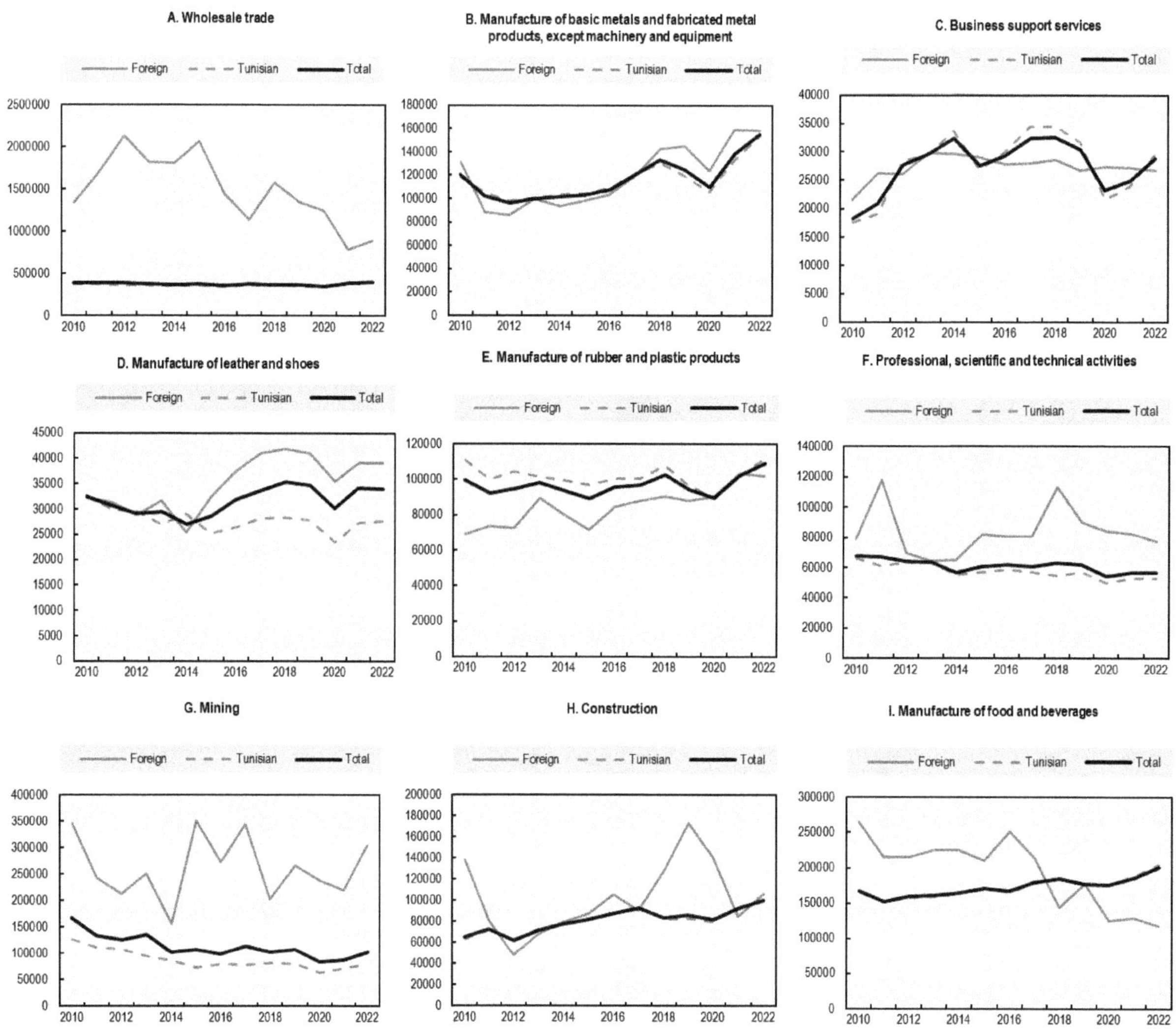

Note: Labour productivity is measured as revenues per employee. Real values were obtained by deflating by the consumer price index. The sectors were selected based on the relative importance in terms of foreign firms' revenues (in addition to sectors shown in figure 2.8).
Source: OECD calculations based on (INS, 2023[13]), the Répertoire National des Entreprises (RNE) sample.

3 FDI impact on job quality and skills

This chapter analyses the potential of foreign direct investment (FDI) to improve labour market outcomes. It assesses the impact of FDI on employment creation and wage conditions across sectors and Tunisian governorates. It also examines how foreign firms in Tunisia contribute to gender equality and skills development, through training practices, but also to reducing possible skills imbalances.

3.1. Summary

An abundant, young and skilled workforce has made Tunisia an attractive destination for foreign direct investment (FDI). The contribution of FDI to labour market outcomes in Tunisia is crucial for an economy where informality and unemployment are high by international standards, particularly among the youth, women, the highly educated and in Tunisia's hinterland regions. As in other countries of the Middle East and North Africa (MENA) region, such as Jordan, stalling business dynamism, combined with skills imbalances, has limited employment opportunities for a steadily increasing and more educated Tunisian labour force. The public sector has absorbed a large number of new graduates and continues to offer attractive working conditions but also limits labour mobility from the public to the private sector.

FDI in Tunisia has strongly contributed to job creation, improved living standards and enhanced skills, but its impact has been uneven across the population and regions. In 2021, one out of five private sector workers were employed in a foreign firm – 34% in manufacturing and 10% in services, among which 95% in foreign offshore firms. Tunisian offshore firms employed 22% of workers in Tunisian companies. The number of workers in foreign firms has doubled since 2005, but many jobs are in low-skilled occupations, created by multinationals exporting automotive components, textiles and clothing, and mechanical and electronics products. Jobs created in services rely more on high-skilled workers, particularly in ICT, business, scientific and technical services, where foreign firms account for 24% to 44% of sectoral employment. Despite attracting half of FDI inflows, jobs created by FDI in the metropolitan area of Tunis – the Grand Tunis – represent 28% of all FDI jobs compared to 34% for the coastal Northeast region.

The job creation intensity of greenfield FDI Tunisia is one the highest of the MENA region – 3.6 jobs created on average for each million of USD invested - and significantly higher than the OECD average. It has also increased in the past decade, partly driven by a shift in FDI to labour-intensive assembling activities of the electronic components sector. Even if most jobs created are in Tunisia's labour-intensive manufacturing activities, job creation from greenfield FDI in some services activities has also expanded in the past decade. Business services, R&D, sales and marketing – activities that may better fit the highly-educated young job seekers – contributed to 12% of new jobs created by greenfield FDI during 2013-2023, twice as much as in 2003-2012. On the other hand, the job creation intensity of FDI in textiles was halved, indicating a sharp decrease in the labour-intensity of the sector due to increased competitive pressures from other emerging markets with lower labour costs.

The job creation performance of FDI in Tunisia has only partly translated into wage and non-wage improvements, which are key to lift standards of living of the population, including women. Foreign firms pay, on average, only marginally higher wages than Tunisian firms, although large variations exist across sectors. Despite increases in recent years, wages in foreign industrial firms continue to be lower than among Tunisian peers as the former operate primarily in low-skilled, low-productivity activities of the automotive equipment and electrics-electronics sectors; exceptions exist in sectors such as minerals, mining, and machine repairing. The impact of foreign firms on gender outcomes is also mixed. The majority of employees in foreign firms are women but these women are mostly employed in low-skilled jobs. Furthermore, foreign firms do not necessarily contribute to improving access of women to managerial roles.

Foreign firms in Tunisia operate in a labour market with large skills imbalances – a misalignment between the demand and supply of skills leading to skills mismatches and shortage, partly stemming from a high number of university graduates and low job creation for the highly skilled. Foreign firms have little impact on improving this imbalance since they operate mostly in sectors relying on low-skilled workers. They also employ fewer skilled workers than foreign firms in other comparator countries. There is scope for skills and knowledge spillovers in the business services sector, as one fourth of firms are foreign. Furthermore, foreign firms are twice as likely to offer training to its employees as Tunisian firms, thereby supporting skills upgrading.

Policy directions

- **Align investment policy and promotion goals with Tunisia Vision 2035 and employment and skills development plans** aiming to boost private sector employment and Tunisia's ambition to become a knowledge-based economy. This implies a balanced approach towards job creation in the investment promotion strategy by continuing to target labour-intensive sectors for job creation, including outside of the Grand Tunis Area, while expanding efforts to target skill-intensive segments of the automotive and electronics sectors' value chains and services sectors such as business services and ICT that support Tunisia's digital transition.
- **Reassess existing restrictions on FDI against objectives of stimulating labour demand in the job-creating, skills-intensive services sectors**. Restrictions on foreign ownership exist in business services, distribution, ICT, tourism, and transports, sectors where FDI has the potential to create jobs for both the low and highly-skilled Tunisian job seekers, including women. Overall, as indicated by the OECD Economic Survey of Tunisia 2022, pursuing pro-competition reforms will contribute to a more dynamic private sector that creates more and better jobs.
- **Improve investment promotion and facilitation efforts based on the existing skills base and labour market potential to lower information barriers for investors.** This includes clear information on labour market characteristics, regulations, existing training programmes and incentives, and supporting investors in identifying suppliers with high labour standards. Tax incentives could support training by firms, including of women and local suppliers. Furthermore, consider introducing pre-employment training programmes to rapidly respond to skills needs of potential new investors or support them establishing their own training facilities.
- **Establish robust monitoring and evaluation mechanisms to effectively assess the impact of FDI on employment and job quality and anticipate skills shortage of foreign firms.** This requires availability and access to representative firm-level statistics, based on the *Répertoire National des Entreprises*, providing information on foreign ownership, employment by gender, wages and non-wage working conditions, and spending on training. This necessitates improving coordination between the INS, FIPA, and APII. Consider involving FIPA in skill needs and anticipation exercises to design and implement active labour market policies and skills development programmes that target the skills needs of foreign firms.

3.2. Key challenges and opportunities for Tunisia's labour market

The Tunisian workforce is young and increasingly educated, but tremendous labour market challenges exist. Unemployment rose from 13% in 2010 to more than 16% in the fourth quarter of 2023; higher than in peer MENA countries, except Jordan (Figure 3.1, panel A). The unemployment rate of the 15-24 year-olds reached 40%. Labour force participation is similar to that of other MENA countries but remains low by international standards: only about half of the working-age population were either in formal employment or actively looking for work in 2019 (Figure 3.1, panel B). This is due to a particularly low labour participation of women, at 28% against 77% for men. A large share of the Tunisian population is in informal employment - almost 40% of total non-agricultural employment - and informality rate exceeded 65% of total employment in sectors such as agriculture, construction, and wholesale and retail trade in 2019 (INS, 2020[1]). Informality is often linked with job insecurity, lack of social security insurance and lower wages, thus contributing to precarity for workers and significant inequalities in the labour market.

3.2.1. Low business dynamism has led to limited employment growth opportunities

Highly educated Tunisian youth and women are facing the greatest challenges on the labour market. The Tunisian population has been growing steadily at a rate of 2% until the mid-1990s, resulting in a rapid expansion of the working-age population (Boughzala, 2019[2]). Rising access to education has improved the education outcomes of women, who make up more than 60% of university graduates. The share of working age population with a tertiary degree has quadrupled since the 1990s, but sluggish growth and low job creation, particularly for educated and skilled workers, have not been sufficient to absorb the increasing number of graduates (OECD, 2022[3]). Among the 25-55 year-olds with tertiary education, 27% were unemployed in 2019, almost twice the national average and one of the highest rates in the MENA region (Kthiri, 2019[4]). The unemployment rate for women with advanced degrees was even higher, at 36%, hampered by cultural gender roles and norms and limited availability of affordable childcare services (World Bank, 2022[5]) (Figure 3.1, panel C). Limited opportunities for youth are particularly concerning as two thirds of the unemployed are under the age of 30. Furthermore, 28% of youth were neither in education nor employment (of which two-thirds were women), a share higher than that of many peer economies and the OECD average of 11% (Figure 3.1, panel D).

Figure 3.1. Labour market conditions in Tunisia

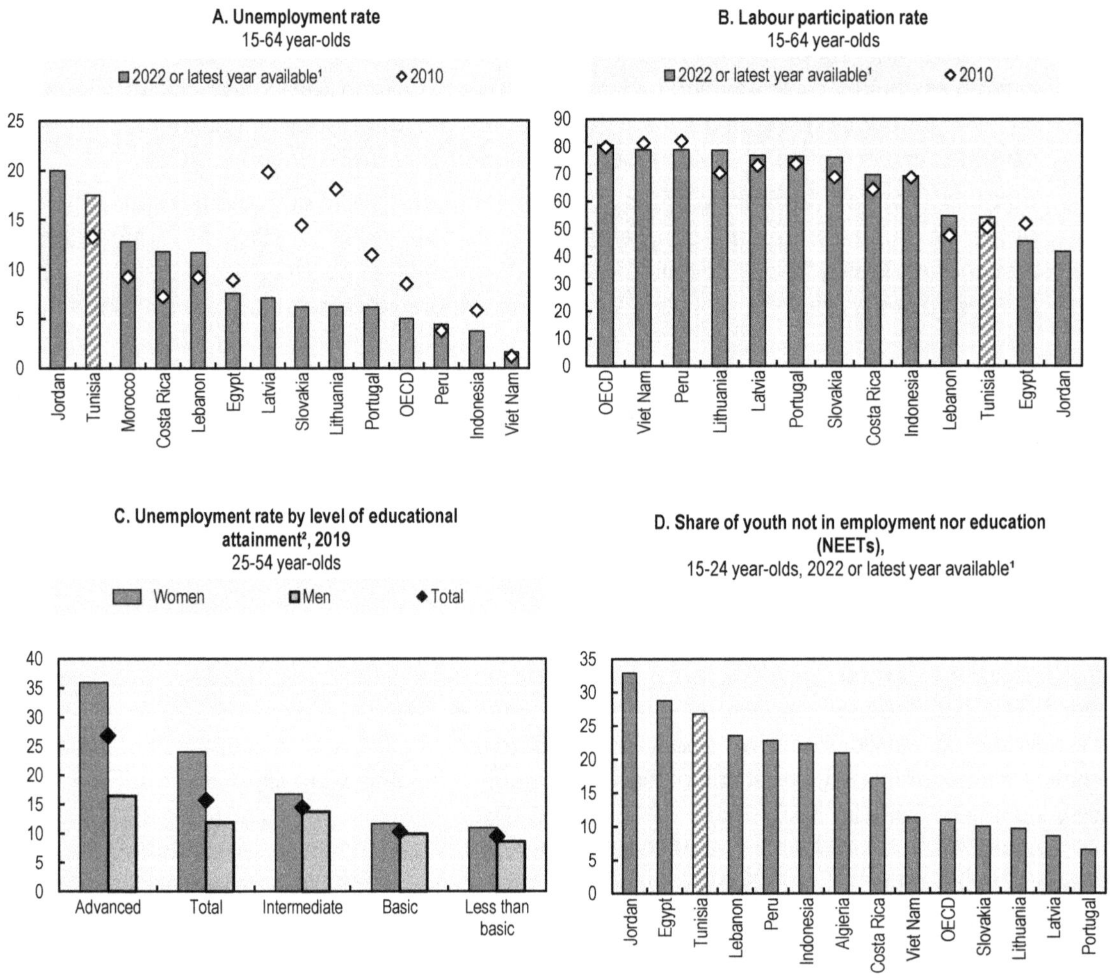

Note: 1. Data refers to 2021 for Egypt, Jordan, Morocco, and 2019 for Lebanon and Tunisia. 2. Advanced: tertiary education; intermediate: upper secondary or post-secondary non-tertiary education; basic: primary and lower secondary education; less than basic: pre-primary education.
Source: ILO Labour Force Statistics (ILO, 2024[6]); OECD Labour Force Statistics, (OECD, 2024[7]), https://stats.oecd.org/

Despite periods of economic growth and important business climate reforms, job creation in Tunisia has been weak due to limited business dynamism and productivity growth, and this particularly affects the highly-educated youth and women (OECD, 2021[8]). Costly and anti-competitive administrative regulations, political uncertainty, and weak incentives to invest limit the entry and exit of firms on the market and hence the efficient reallocation of resources (see Chapter 2). Further reforms to improve product market competition, together with increased labour market flexibility, would improve business dynamism and help create formal jobs (Belgacem and Vacher, 2023[9]). Many Tunisian firms are small, often micro-enterprises that offer low-skilled and low-paid jobs, and the labour market lacks high-end jobs for the increasing number highly skilled workers (Boughzala, 2019[2]). The increasing number of graduates with tertiary education and the lack of adequate employment opportunities exacerbate the existing skills imbalances on the labour market.

3.2.2. *Job creation has been uneven across sectors and regions*

Many of the jobs in Tunisia are in low-productivity sectors with low-skilled employment. The services sector is the largest employer, with more than one fourth of jobs in either transport, repair, tourism, or retail (Figure). Retail trade and the construction sector were the main sectors driving employment growth since 2007 (OECD, 2022[3]). The more productive banking and insurance sector accounts for only 2% of services employment and 1% of total employment. Manufacturing jobs in textiles, mechanical and electrical industries, and food and beverages, combined, make up three-quarters of all manufacturing employment (Figure 3.2). These sectors, while important for employment, rely mostly on jobs requiring intermediate or basic educational attainments and offer modest wages. Employment growth in the mechanical and electrical industries was the main contributor to employment growth in manufacturing since 2007, while the relative importance of textiles declined.

Figure 3.2. Employment in Tunisia is concentrated mostly in services

Share of employment by broad sectors, 2019

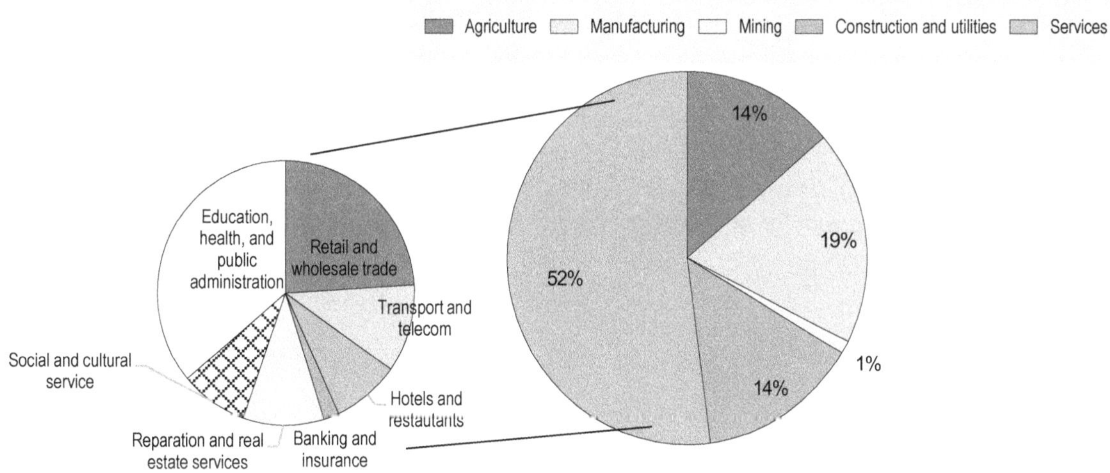

Source: INS, (2024[10]), https://ins.tn/statistiques/151 .

Despite limited productivity growth, the public sector has expanded in the past decade on the back of hiring expansion and wage increases. Employment in the public sector makes up about one-fifth of total employment and attracts highly educated youth and women – public administration has absorbed most of the university graduates since 2007 and has contributed significantly to overall employment growth (OECD,

2022[3]). While jobs in the public sector do not necessarily offer better starting salaries to recent graduates, many of these graduates find such jobs attractive because of additional benefits such as job security, guaranteed pay increases, long maternity leave or flexible working hours (World Bank, 2022[5]).

Unequal private sector development across regions has also contributed to disparities in the labour market, with unemployment ranging from below 10% in some coastal governorates to almost 30% in some southern and western regions. Mountainous and rural regions in the west and south face limited non-agricultural employment opportunities, especially for skilled workers (Boughzala and Hamdi, 2014[11]). The Northeast and Central East coastal regions have traditionally attracted labour-intensive economic activities thanks to their strategic location for maritime export, investments in infrastructure and the development of industrial clusters. While this has helped reduce unemployment, employers still struggle to find an adequate workforce in many sectors due to limited labour mobility across regions related to structural and cultural factors (OECD, 2022[3]).

3.3. The contribution of FDI to employment

3.3.1. Foreign companies employ one out of five workers in the private sector

Trade and investment liberalisation, the creation of the “offshore regime”, and a competitive and abundant labour force have contributed to attracting FDI with large consequences on firm and employment dynamics in Tunisia. The share of employment in foreign companies has been expanding, rising from 13% of formal private sector employment in 2005 to 21% in 2021 (Figure 3.3, panel A). Compared to other countries, this share is similar to the OECD average but lower than in some small open economies such as Czechia, Slovakia or Ireland (Figure 3.3, panel B). In absolute terms, private sector employment in foreign firms doubled between 2005 and 2021, while employment in domestic firms grew by 20%. Over 200 000 workers were employed in foreign companies in 2021, across all economic sectors.

Foreign presence has been prominent in manufacturing, with 34% of private sector employment in foreign companies in 2022, in contrast with services where this share was 10% (Figure 3.3, panel A). In some manufacturing sectors that have attracted large amounts of FDI, foreign firms account for at least 45% of employment – namely automotive components, leather and shoes, and mechanical and electronics (Figure 3.3, panel C). Combined, these sectors represent around 15% of total private sector employment and 31% of manufacturing employment. Foreign manufacturers’ contribution to employment in the food industry is low while the sector creates many jobs – the food sector is strongly regulated and has a large presence of SOEs (World Bank, 2014[12]). In the services sector, foreign firms’ presence is largest in ICT, business support services, and scientific and technical services, where they account for 24% to 44% of sectoral employment (INS, 2022[13]). Overall, services sectors are more restrictive to FDI than manufacturing. For instance, foreign firms account for about 1% of employment in transport and storage, tourism, education, and health.

Figure 3.3. Share of employment in foreign companies

% of foreign firms in total private sector employment

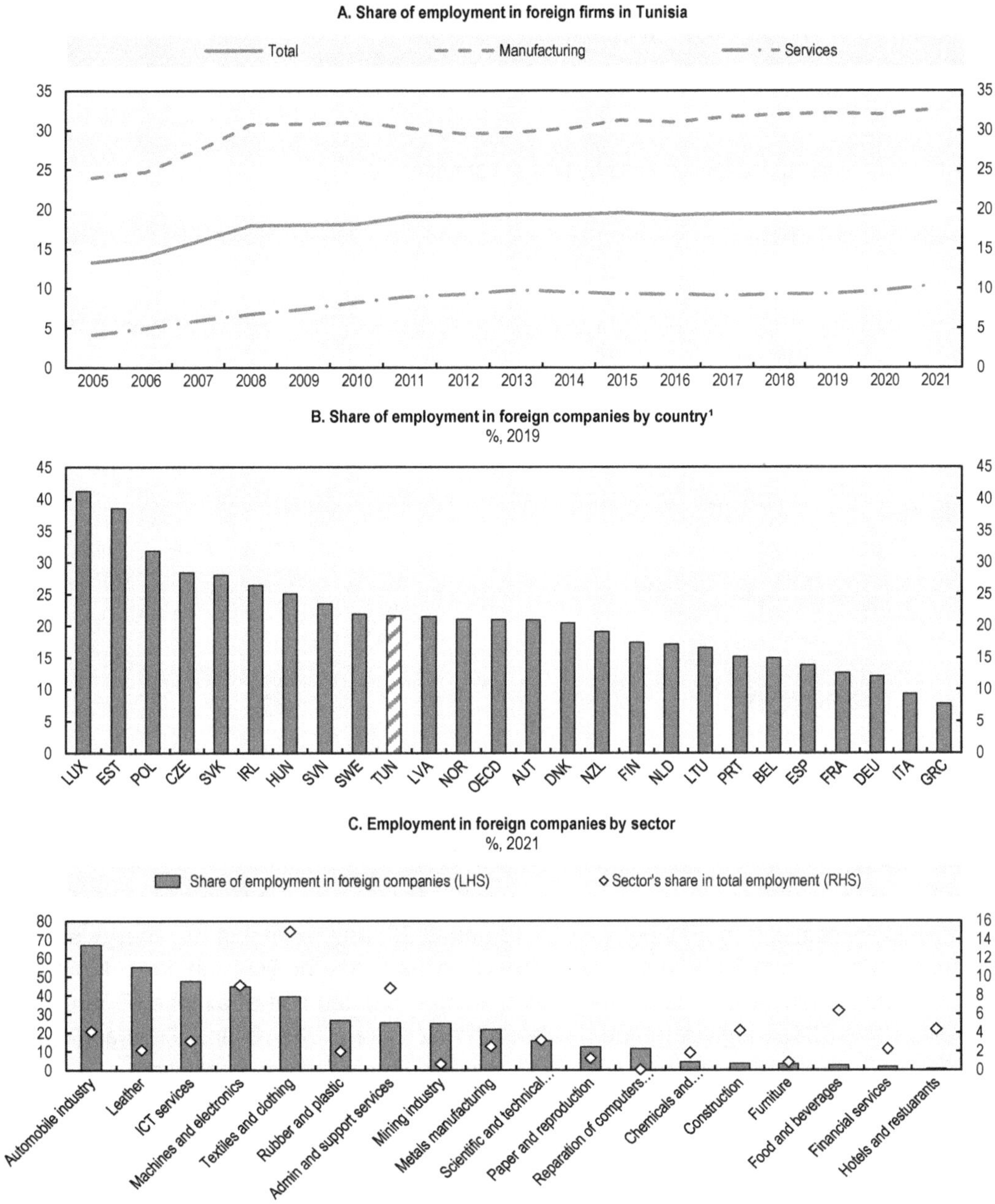

Note: Data in all figures refers to private sector employment. 1. For reasons of data comparability, country aggregates exclude agriculture, financial and insurance activities, education services, healthcare, arts, entertainment and recreation, other services, and public administration (corresponding to ISIC rev. 4 sectors B-N, excluding K).
Source: OECD calculations based on (INS, 2023[14]) Répertoire National des Entreprises; and (OECD, 2023[15]), OECD AMNE Database, https://www.oecd.org/sti/ind/analytical-amne-database.htm.

The majority of foreign manufacturers operate under the offshore regime, meaning that they export nearly all their production (see Chapter 2 for more analysis on the interlinkages between FDI and the offshore regime in Tunisia). In 2021, among the group of foreign firms, those in the offshore sector employed 95% of workers while representing 79% of the group, in stark contrast with Tunisian offshore firms that employed 22% of workers in Tunisian companies (Figure 3.4).Offshore companies play a critical role in shaping labour market outcomes in Tunisia, accounting for almost 40% of total private sector employment in 2021, although they represent only 4% of all firms. This discrepancy highlights the significant interlinkages and potential dependencies created by the offshore regime between trade, investment and employment outcomes in Tunisia. The large concentration of employment in offshore companies, makes jobs more vulnerable to global trade and economic turbulences.

Figure 3.4. Job creation by foreign companies create occurs mostly under the offshore regime

Share of employment in Tunisian and foreign firms by type of company, 2021

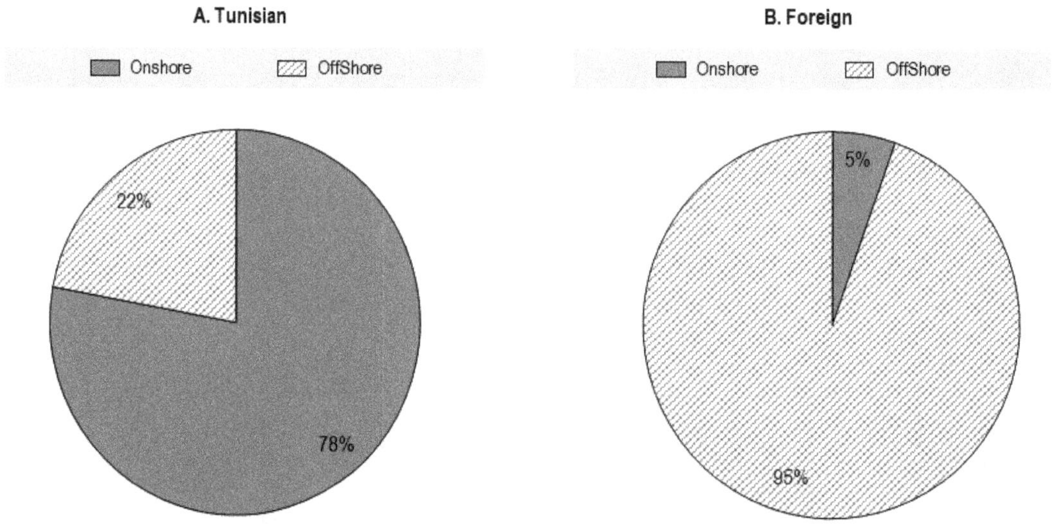

Source: OECD based on, (INS, 2023[14]), Répertoire National des Entreprises.

3.3.2. FDI-related job creation strongly varies across sectors and regions

Over the past decade, there has been a large concentration of jobs created from FDI in manufacturing. Out of all the new jobs created from FDI between 2013 and 2022, and excluding the energy sector, over 90% were in manufacturing and 6.5% in services. The opposite holds for Tunisian firms. Moreover, two manufacturing sectors – electronics and textiles and clothing – created half of all jobs (Figure 3.5). One third of jobs created from FDI during that period was in electronics alone. This reflects the changing sectoral distribution of FDI in Tunisia and a shift to more labour-intensive manufacturing activities.

Figure 3.5. The distribution of jobs created from FDI in Tunisia by sector

Share of jobs created from FDI as a % of total jobs created (excluding energy), 2013-2022

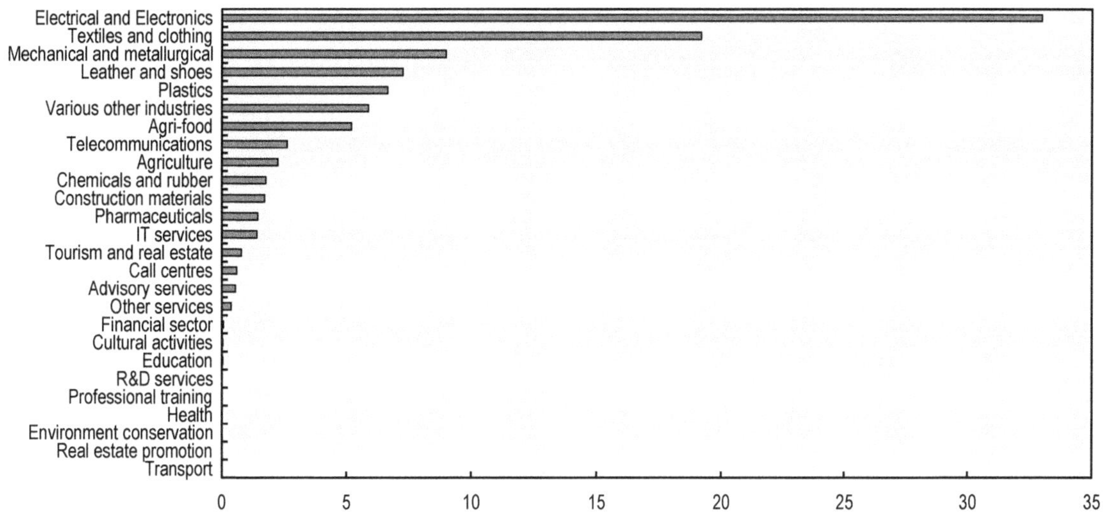

Source: OECD based on Foreign Investment Promotion Agency (FIPA, 2023[16]).

The benefits of FDI in terms of employment are not shared equally across regions and reflect the large regional disparities in foreign investment, as is the case in other countries (OECD, 2022[17]). However, these benefits are geographically more evenly distributed than FDI itself. The Tunis governorate attracted 31% of FDI flows between 2013 and 2022 and the metropolitan area of Tunis – the Grand Tunis – more than half of FDI flows (Figure 3.6, Panel A). At the same time, the share of jobs created from FDI was 9% in Tunis governorate and 28% in the Grand Tunis (Figure 3.6, Panel B). Foreign projects in the agglomeration of Tunis are more geared towards services and, in turn, less labour-intensive than in regions with stronger manufacturing activity. Most foreign companies are located in the Grand Tunis region and this could have had positive spillovers for job creation in the neighbouring regions. Previous studies on Tunisia have found evidence of agglomeration effects where FDI inflows in one region create some positive spillovers in nearby regions (Bouzid and Toumi, 2020[18]). However, it is not the southern governorates, where unemployment is highest, that have benefited the most from FDI. The coastal Northeast and Centre East regions accounted respectively for 34% and 25% of jobs created from FDI between 2013 and 2022. Access to ports and a good road network have proved essential to attract job-creating, export-oriented, manufacturing FDI in Tunisia's textiles and automotive sectors.

Figure 3.6. Disparity in job creation from FDI across Tunisian governorates

Share by governorate in the total 2013-2022 FDI stock (excluding energy)

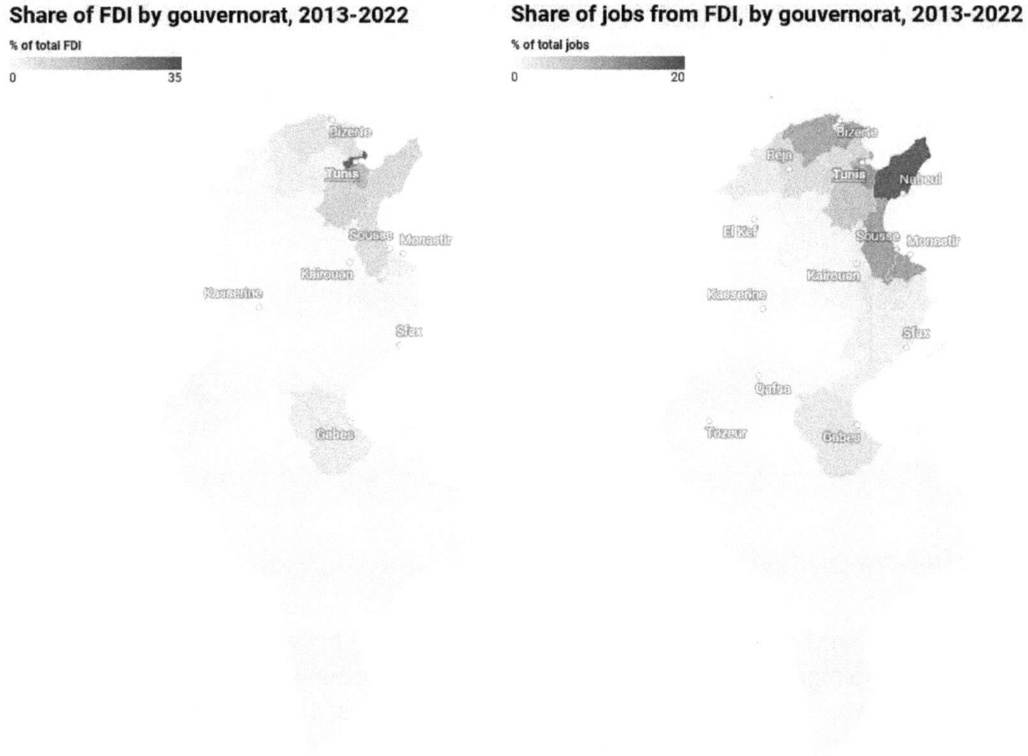

Source: OECD calculations based on Foreign Investment Promotion Agency (FIPA, 2023[16]).

3.3.3. The job creation intensity of greenfield FDI has increased over the past decade

Employment from FDI in Tunisia inherently reflects the scale of foreign investment at the national level and its distribution across sectors. It is also the consequence of the job creation intensity of FDI, which provides an indication of the "value-for-money" impact of FDI on employment in the host country. From a policy perspective, investment promotion agencies, including Tunisia's FIPA, dedicate ample resources to attracting greenfield FDI with the hope that it creates ample employment (OECD, 2021[8]). In Tunisia, each million USD of greenfield FDI announced between 2003 and 2022 is expected to have created 3.6 direct jobs on average, twice the average of the MENA region and significantly above the OECD average (Figure 3.7). The job creation intensity increased in the past decade with respect to years 2003-2012, as a result of FDI activity shifting away from capital-intensive mining towards labour-intensive manufacturing activities. However, this impact remains lower than in other small open economies such as Costa Rica, Lithuania and Slovakia.

Figure 3.7. Job creation intensity of greenfield FDI in Tunisia and comparator countries

Direct jobs created per mln USD of FDI invested, 2003-2022

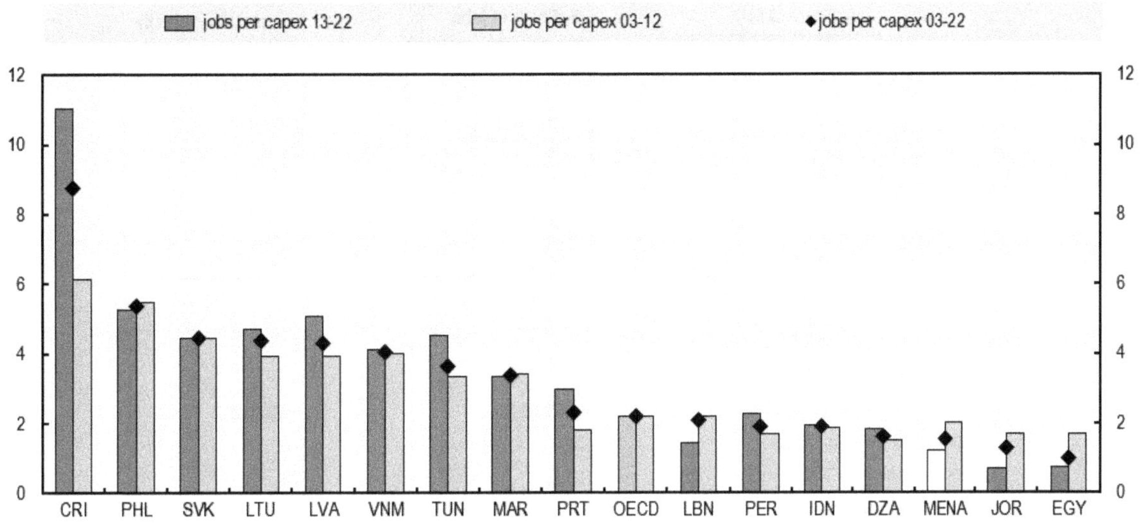

Note: Data includes the energy sector.
Source: OECD calculation based on (Financial Times, 2024[19]) fDi Markets Database, https://www.fdimarkets.com.

Tunisia's strong job creation intensity of FDI relies on a few highly labour-intensive activities, indicating that modest changes in the distribution of investment can have large impact on job creation prospects. Over 2013-2022, sectors that attracted the most FDI were not necessarily those where job creation was greatest. The energy sector, which is excluded from FIPA's statistics, real estate, and hotel and tourism, accounted together for two-thirds of FDI but only 18% of new jobs created from FDI (Figure 3.8, Panel A and B). The textiles and automotive industries created nearly 40% of jobs from FDI despite attracting only 6% of FDI. This illustrates striking differences in the job creation intensity across sectors, which varies from 0.25 jobs per million of USD invested in fossil fuel energy to 38 jobs in the business machines and equipment sector. Greenfield FDI in textiles and electronics created at least 30 new jobs per million USD and has been an important source of employment creation in Tunisia (Figure 3.8, Panel C).

The job creation intensity of greenfield FDI in Tunisia has even increased in the past decade, indicating a structural shift in the composition of foreign investment both across and within sectors, i.e. in the type of activity. Job intensity can increase either through greater labour-intensity of activities within sectors or more FDI going towards labour-intensive sectors. Within sectors, while changes in the job creation intensity of FDI were limited in many sectors attracting big shares of FDI between the periods 2003-2012 and 2013-2022, there has been a shift within the most job-intensive sectors (Figure 3.9). The electronic components and consumer electronics sector were the two sectors with the highest job creation intensity in 2013-2022, each nearly doubling their job creation intensity with respect to the previous decade, suggesting a surge in labour-intensive activities within these sectors. On the other hand, the job creation intensity of the textiles sector was halved, indicating significantly lower labour-intensity as the sector faces increasing competitiveness pressures from other emerging markets (Ministère de l'Industrie, 2022[20]).

Figure 3.8. Contribution of greenfield FDI to job creation in Tunisia

Shares of greenfield FDI and jobs and job creation intensity, 2013-2022

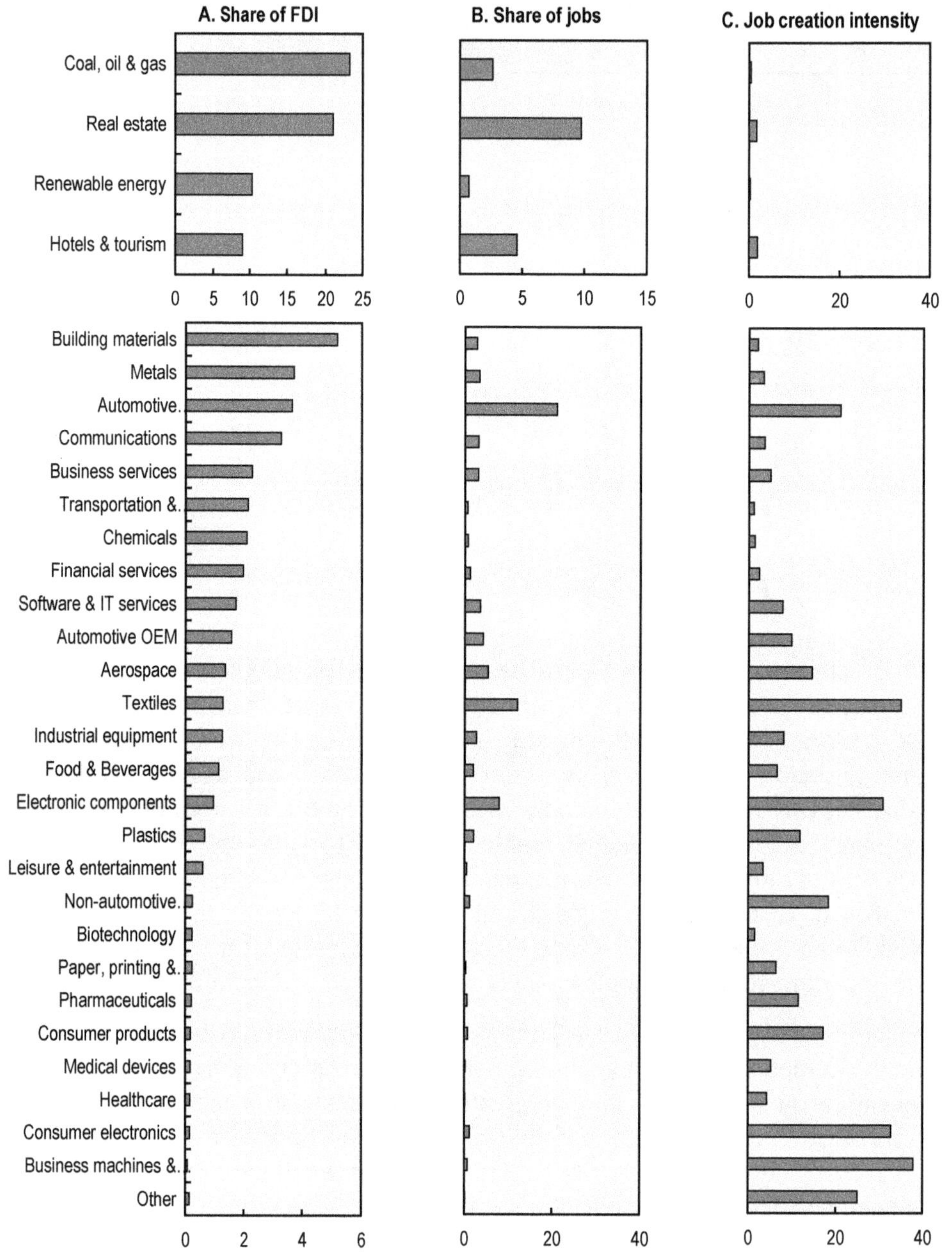

Note: Many of the reported jobs created are estimates, The sectoral composition may differ from figure 3.5 due to differences in sector classification between the databases.
Source: OECD calculation based on (Financial Times, 2024[19]) fDi Markets Database, https://www.fdimarkets.com.

Figure 3.9. Job creation intensity of greenfield FDI changes over time and by sector

Jobs created per mln of USD, 2003-2012 and 2013-2022

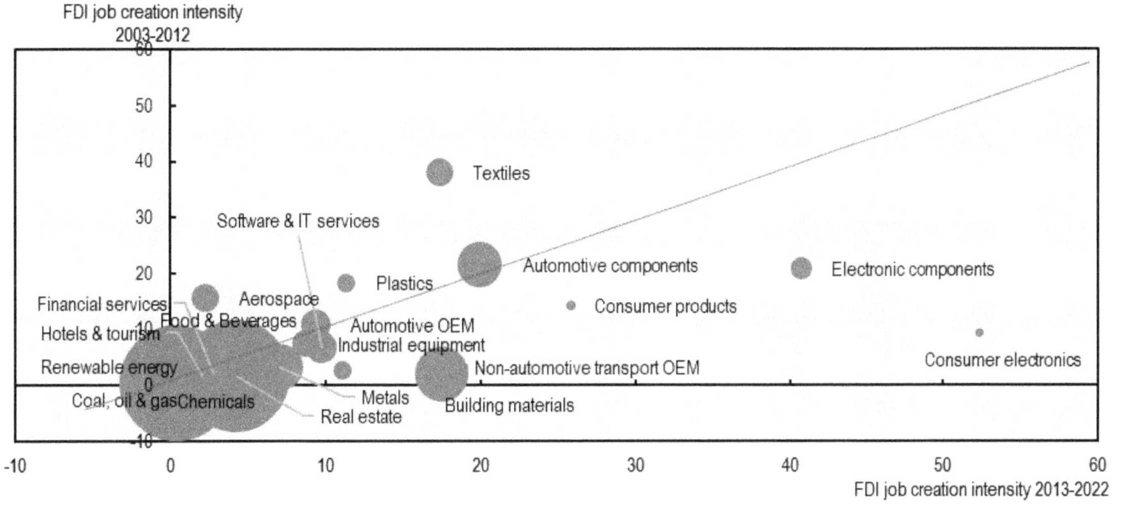

Note: The size of the bubble reflects the sector's share in total FDI during 2003-2022.
Source: OECD calculation based on (Financial Times, 2024[19]) fDi Markets Database, https://www.fdimarkets.com.

Sectoral shifts in greenfield FDI are interlinked with the changes in the type of activity of FDI projects between 2003-2012 and 2013-2023. While manufacturing and construction activities made up 80% of all FDI-related activities during the two periods, their relative shares changed substantially (Figure 3.10, panels A and B). The importance of construction decreased significantly because of a drop in FDI in the real estate sector, whereas the share of jobs from manufacturing activities increased on the back of a surge in FDI-related job creation in the electronics sector. Manufacturing has also been a key, if not the only, activity in the automotive and textiles sectors (Figure 3.10, panels C and D). This is typical of countries that receive labour-intensive FDI and similar patterns have been observed in peer countries (OECD, 2021[8]). Interestingly, there has been an increased importance of services activities. Business services, R&D, and sales and marketing activities contributed to 12% of new jobs created during 2013-2023, in contrast to 6% in the previous period (Figure 3.10, panels A and B). R&D was prominent in the software & IT services sector, where they contributed to 54% on new jobs created from FDI (Figure 3.10, panel E). At the same time, it was driven by the presence of one very job-intensive FDI project and does not necessarily define a trend in the sector.

Figure 3.10. Share of jobs created from greenfield FDI by type of activity

Share of jobs created from greenfield FDI, by type of activity

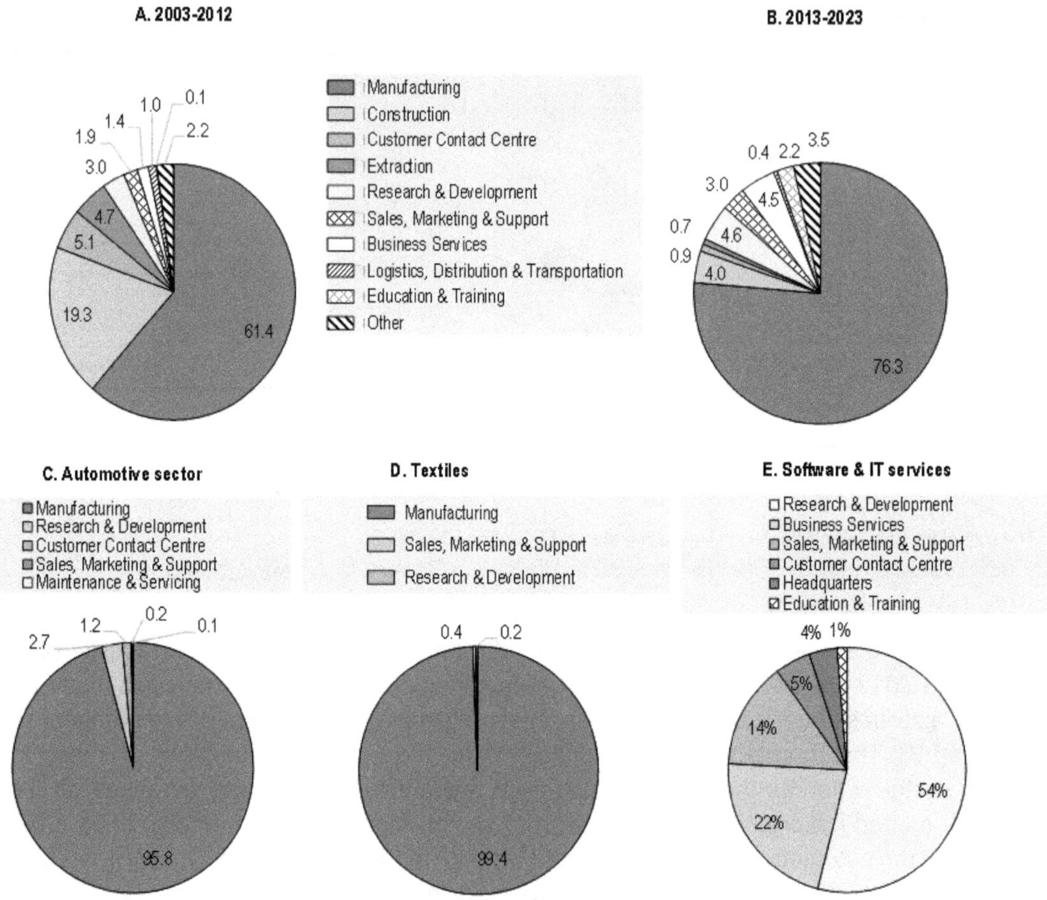

Note: Greenfield FDI corresponds to announced capital expenditure (CAPEX). Number of jobs and CAPEX are partly based on estimates.
Source: OECD calculations based on (Financial Times, 2024[19]) FDI Markets database, https://www.fdimarkets.com.

3.4. The contribution of FDI to job quality and gender outcomes

Beyond job creation, FDI influences wage and non-wage working conditions, including job stability, safety, and employment conditions, as well as gender outcomes on the labour market (OECD, 2022[21]). Foreign firms also influence employer-worker relations. As an adherent to the OECD Guidelines on Multinational Enterprises, Tunisian authorities are required to promote the Guidelines and perform related due diligence. The Guidelines provide several clauses related to workers' rights, industrial relations and ensuring workers' safety (Box 2.1). Overall, labour market institutions are crucial to ensure that FDI does not contribute to deteriorating working conditions. Collective bargaining and workers' voice arrangements can particularly help ensure that workers benefit from FDI by supporting collective solutions to emerging issues and conflicts (OECD, 2022[21]). This section focuses the contribution of FDI to wage and gender outcomes.

Box 3.1. OECD Guidelines for Multinational Enterprises: Employment and Industrial Relations

MNEs should, within the framework of applicable law, regulations and prevailing labour relations and employment practices and applicable international labour standards:

- Respect the right of workers employed by the MNE to establish or join trade unions and representative organisations of their own choosing.
- Observe standards of employment and industrial relations not less favourable than those observed by comparable employers in the host country. Where comparable employers may not exist, provide the best possible wages and conditions of work, within the framework of government policies.
- To the greatest extent practicable, employ local workers and provide training, in co-operation with worker representatives and, where appropriate, relevant governmental authorities.
- Take adequate steps to ensure occupational health and safety in their operations.
- In considering changes in their operations which would have major employment effects, provide reasonable notice of such changes to representatives of the workers, and, where appropriate, to the relevant governmental authorities, and co-operate to mitigate practicable adverse effects.
- In the context of bona fide negotiations with workers' representatives on conditions of employment, or while workers are exercising a right to organise, not threaten to transfer activity in order to influence unfairly those negotiations or to hinder the exercise of a right to organise.

The Guidance sets out practical ways to help businesses avoid potential negative impacts of their activities and their supply chains. It aims to bolster policy efforts to strengthen confidence between enterprises and the societies in which they operate, and complements both the due diligence recommendations contained in the *UN Guiding Principles on Business and Human Rights* and the *ILO Declaration on Fundamental Principles and Rights at Work*.

Source: OECD (2023[22]), OECD Guidelines for Multinational Enterprises on Responsible Business Conduct, OECD Publishing, Paris, https://doi.org/10.1787/81f92357-en.

3.4.1. Foreign firms pay increasingly higher wages than Tunisian firms in the services sector

The economic performance of Tunisia in the past two decades has not gone hand in hand with strong improvements in wages which is key for lifting living standards. Despite nominal wages growing at an average rate of over 5% since 2000, average earnings in Tunisia are well below those of peer OECD and non-OECD countries (Figure 3.11, panel A). The monthly minimum wage in the non-agricultural sectors (*Salaire minimum interprofessionnel garanti*) was 390 Tunisian dinars (around 125 dollars) in 2022; a low level by international standards. Wages vary across sectors, with the highest earnings observed in finance, mining, and ICT services, which is due to the higher value added and higher productivity of these sectors (see Chapter 2) (Figure 3.11, panel B). Earnings in the manufacturing sector are below the national average, as jobs in the manufacturing sector in Tunisia usually require only basic skills. Competitive wages, combined with a growing labour market and proximity to European markets, have been important factors for FDI attractiveness in Tunisia.

Figure 3.11. Wages in Tunisia are low compared to those of peer countries

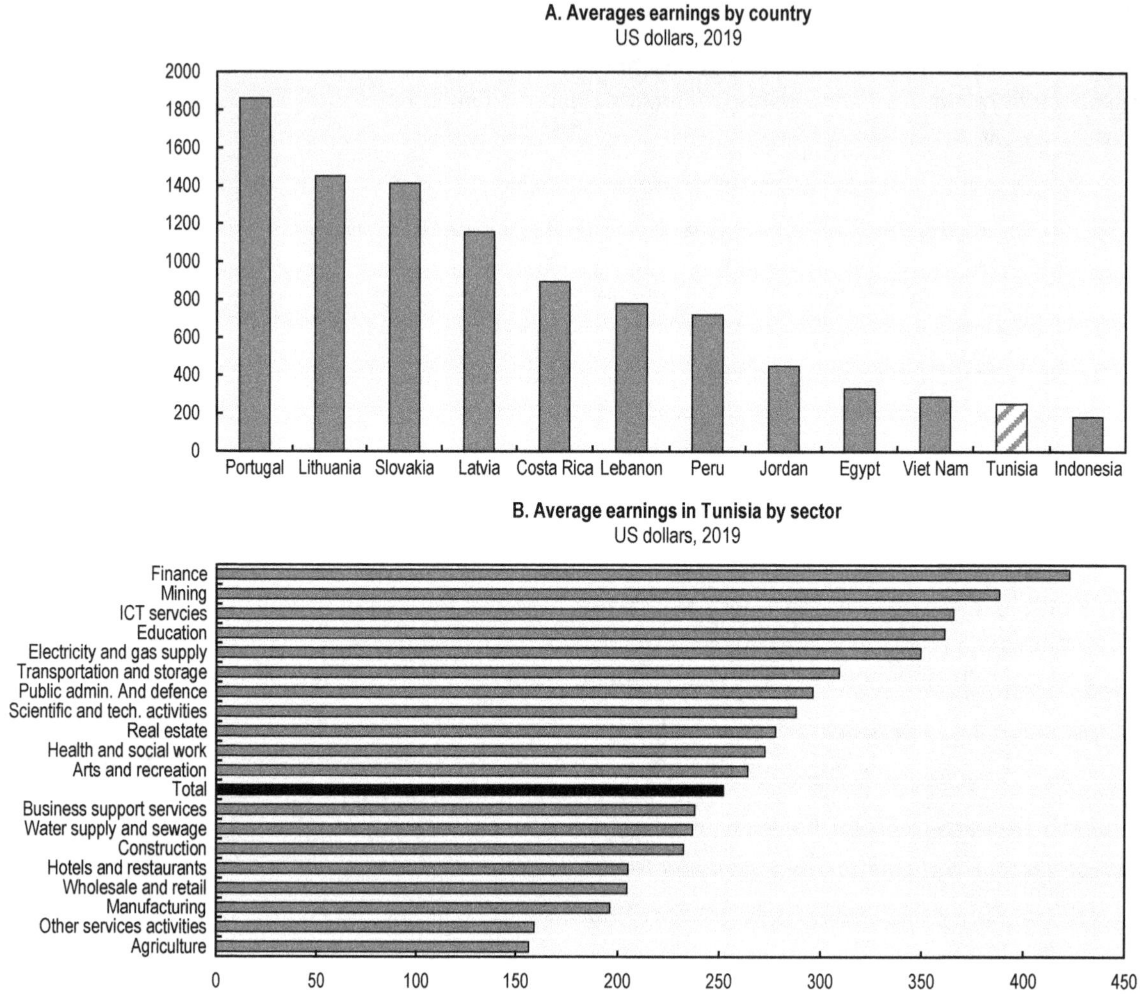

Source: (ILO, 2024[23]), Statistics on wages, https://ilostat.ilo.org/topics/wages/.

Increased FDI to Tunisia has contributed to improved working conditions, notably through higher wages, although the benefits have varied across sectors and may not have been felt by all segments of the population. The positive impacts of FDI might not materialise if for example foreign firms engage in irresponsible business practices or attract skilled workers away from domestic firms (OECD, 2022[21]). As foreign companies are often larger and more productive, they typically offer better wages, but the extent to which this outcome materialises largely depends on the sector where firms operate (OECD, 2019[24]). For example, firms operating in low-value added manufacturing sectors that rely on low-skilled workers have less of a margin for providing better wages than firms in high-tech manufacturing industries. Yet, excessive wage dispersions between foreign and domestic firms can also lead to increased wage inequalities. As Tunisia heavily attracts FDI in low value-added manufacturing sectors or activities, the economy-wide impact has been limited.

The foreign wage premium, which measures average wages per worker in foreign companies relative to domestic ones, has increased since 2010, albeit from negative levels. Average wages in foreign firms had been lower in the past, but increases in recent years led to the wage premium turning positive in 2020 (Figure 3.12, Panel A). In 2022, wages in foreign firms were on average 3% higher than in Tunisian firms, but a large discrepancy exists between wages in manufacturing and services sectors. In particular, the services sector experienced a significant increase after 2017, with the foreign wage premium doubling between 2010 and 2022, driven by increasing foreign wage premia in business services, professional and scientific activities and the computer repairs sector. In 2022, foreign firms paid almost 60% higher wages than domestic firms in services.

Services sectors where foreign firms paid higher wages than Tunisian firms include repair of computers and machines, and wholesale and retail trade (Figure 3.12, Panel B). In these sectors, foreign firms offered wages that were at least twice as high as those of Tunisian firms throughout the period 2010-2022. Repair of computers was the sector with the highest foreign wage premium of 310% but, at the same time, where only 1% of all companies are foreign. It suggests that there are a few large foreign companies that pay high wages, whereas many domestic firms are probably small micro firms with relatively low wages. Furthermore, foreign firms exhibit positive wage premia in two services sectors where they are strongly present – ICT services and business support services, which together account for almost a third of the total foreign wage bill and contributed to the rapid increase in the foreign wage premium in services. These sectors tend to be more skill-intensive. In turn, the foreign wage premium may partly reflect a skill premium.

In the manufacturing sector, despite slight increases in recent years, wages in foreign companies were, on average, lower than in Tunisian firms (Figure 3.12, Panel A). Some key sectors display a negative foreign wage premium, including food and beverages, chemicals and pharmaceuticals, automotive equipment, and mechanical and electronics (Figure 3.12, Panel B). Foreign firms may be motivated to invest in Tunisia's manufacturing sectors due to comparatively low labour costs and hence would not have the incentive or margin to improve the wage conditions of their workers. It is also a reflection of the relatively lower labour productivity of foreign firms in the manufacturing sectors in Tunisia vis-à-vis domestic firms, such as in automobiles and electronics (see Chapter 2). At the same time, mining, metals, and machine equipment repair had strong foreign wage premia in 2022, reflecting the higher value-added of activities in these sectors. Nevertheless, these sectors account for a small share of the activity of foreign firms and contributed little to the overall wage premium. The significant differences in foreign wage premia across sectors, might suggest the cost-competitiveness motivation of foreign firms to invest in a particular sector.

The foreign wage premium in Tunisia is low in comparison with the OECD average and some peer economies. Comparable data across selected countries, which covers primarily the manufacturing industry, shows that, in many countries, foreign firms pay higher wages than domestic ones, resulting in a positive foreign wage premium in these countries (Figure 3.13). However, in Tunisia the foreign wage premium was at around 0, while in OECD countries wages in foreign firms in the manufacturing sector are on average 40% higher than in domestic ones. This indicator varies slightly from the indicators in Figure 3.12, because of differences in sector coverages across the databases. It reflects the fact that foreign firms in Tunisia, like in Jordan or Thailand, are not significantly more productive than domestic firms or may be concentrated in sectors with more competitive labour costs.

Figure 3.12. Wage premium of foreign firms in Tunisia across sectors

Wage premium of foreign firms by sector, average wages for 2010-2022

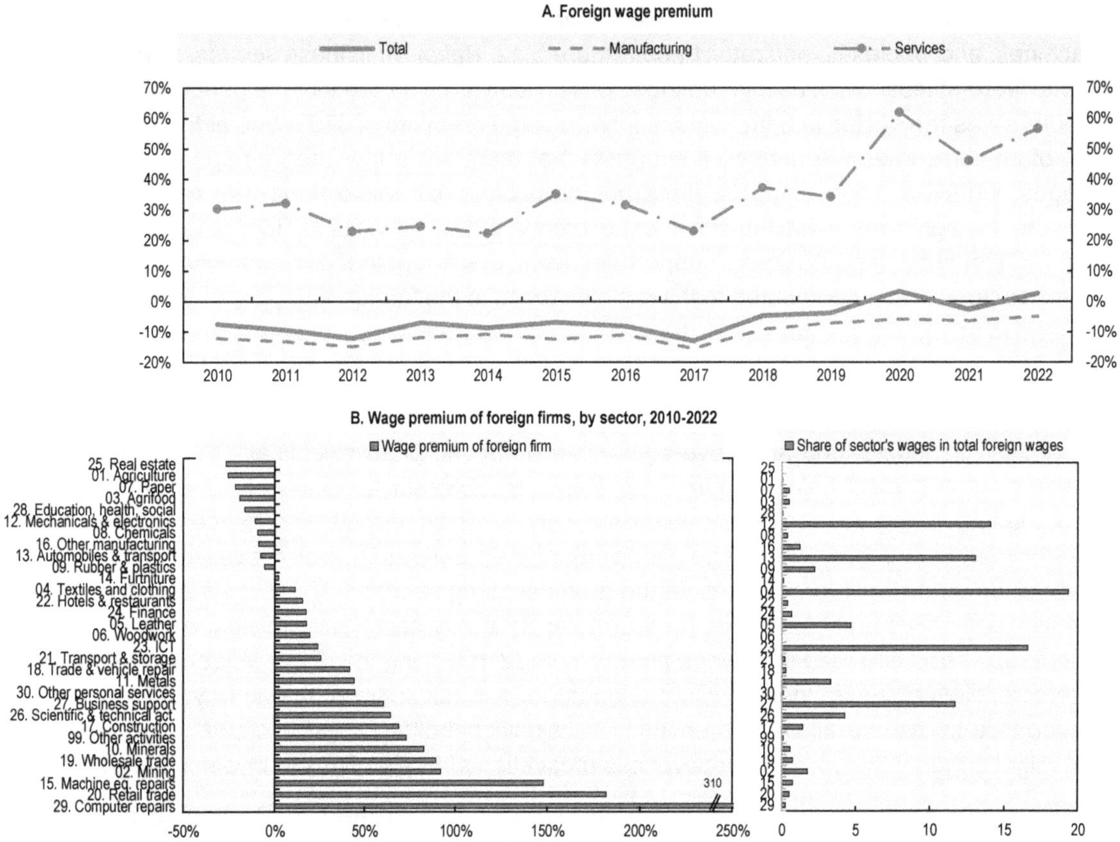

Note: Panel A excludes agriculture, construction, and the trade sectors where informal employment is most prevalent.
Source: OECD calculations based on (INS, 2023[14]), the Répertoire National des Entreprises (RNE) sample.

Figure 3.13. Average wage premium of foreign firms

Foreign firms pay higher wages if index >0, 2020 or latest year available

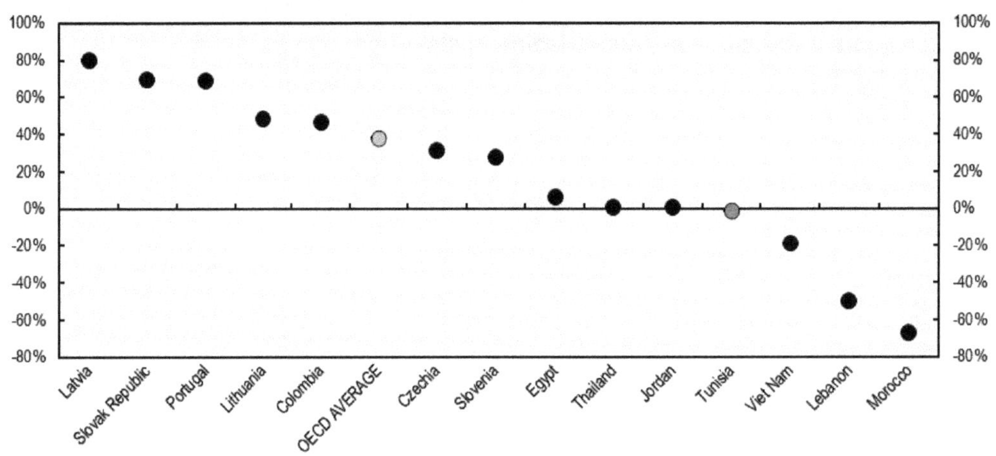

Note: The World Bank Enterprise Survey for Tunisia and other economies is based on a sample of firms and includes primarily manufacturing sectors, with a strong representation of food and beverages, and textile and clothing industry.
Source: OECD calculations based on (World Bank, 2024[25]), World Bank Enterprise Survey.

3.4.2. Foreign firms pay higher wages in sectors where they are more productive

Despite different trends of foreign labour productivity (Chapter 2) and wage premia, there is a positive correlation between premia at the sector level. Taking average premia for 2010-2022, sectors with higher labour productivity premia are more likely to offer higher wage premia, but the relationship is not proportional (Figure 3.14). It shows that improvements in labour productivity are an important catalyst for better wage benefits for workers, as foreign firms are usually larger, more technologically advanced, and hire more skilled workers (OECD, 2019[26]). In a sector with foreign firms are twice as productive as domestic ones, those firms pay 70% higher wages on average. Sectors where this relationship is the most prominent include financial services, mining, minerals and metals, scientific and technical activities, and other personal services. At the same time, there are notable exceptions – for example, in retail trade, there is no foreign labour productivity premium while foreign firms pay 200% more on average. Conversely, while foreign firms in wholesale trade are three times as productive as domestic ones on average, this translates to 90% higher wages. Nevertheless, as shown before, numbers in these sectors are likely to display anomalies and must be interpreted with caution.

Figure 3.14. The foreign wage premium is positively correlated with labour productivity premium

Average of 2010-2022 by sector

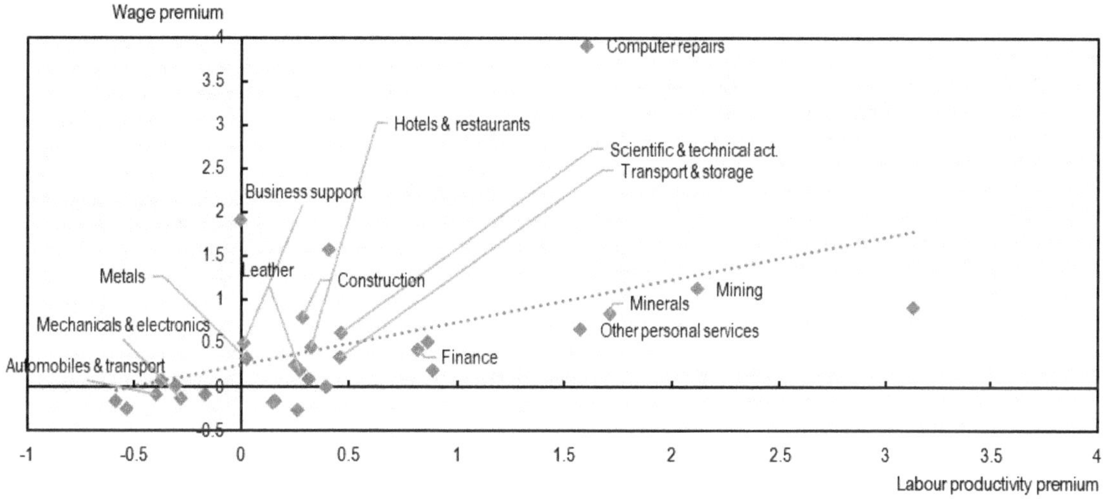

Note: The dotted line represents the linear trend.
Source: OECD calculations based on (INS, 2023[14]), the Répertoire National des Entreprises (RNE) sample.

3.4.3. Foreign firms employ more women than Tunisian firms but not in managerial positions

FDI can also contribute to improvements in labour market outcomes through increased female labour participation, which could be important in countries like Tunisia where female labour participation is relatively low. Tunisian women are employed throughout all sectors of the economy, but there is a strong tendency for them to work in agriculture, public services, as well as textiles and electric and electronic industries (Boughzala, 2019[2]) – two manufacturing sectors with a strong presence of foreign firms. Female employment in manufacturing sectors is relatively high in Tunisia compared to peer MENA and OECD countries and is even higher among foreign firms; albeit the jobs are often in low-skilled occupations (Figure 3.15, panel A). Women make up 58% of workers in foreign firms on average, in contrast to 37% in domestic firms, as FDI in Tunisia is increasingly directed at sectors where female employment has been traditionally higher. On the other hand, domestic firms are more concentrated in the services sectors such as retail and transport, where male employment is more prevalent (Boughzala, 2019[2])).

Despite the high share of female employees, women rarely reach top managerial positions in Tunisia, like in other MENA countries. Only 10% of firms have a female top manager, with the share slightly higher in domestic firms (Figure 3.15, panel B). Results vary across countries, with the share of firms having female managers varying from 2% in Jordan to 65% in Thailand. In Tunisia, there still seems to be a glass ceiling for female promotion that is also present in foreign firms. Nevertheless, it is more common for women to participate in the firm's ownership. Female participation in ownership is a characteristic in 40% of domestic firms and 36% of foreign firms, similarly to the OECD average and much higher than in other MENA countries (Figure 3.15, panel C).

Figure 3.15. Foreign firms' contribution to gender outcomes is limited

Percentage, 2020 or latest year available

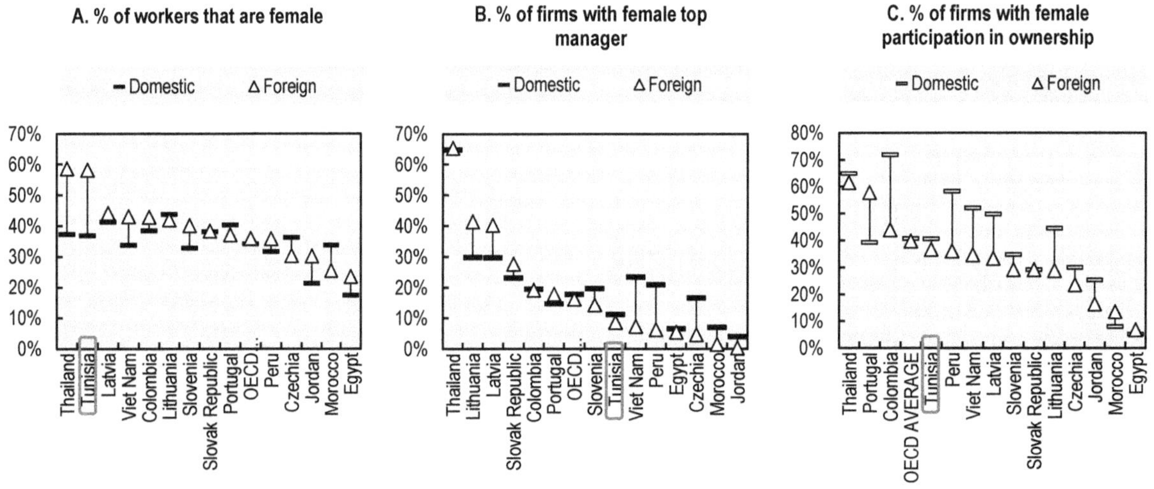

Source: OECD calculations based on (World Bank, 2024[25]), World Bank Enterprise Survey, https://www.enterprisesurveys.org/en/data.

3.5. The contribution of FDI to skills development

3.5.1. Tunisian workforce is mainly employed in low-skilled jobs

Despite a diversified economy, most of the jobs in Tunisia are in low-productivity sectors and predominantly low-skilled occupations. In part, this is a consequence of past economic policies to attract low value-added activities based on competitive labour costs such as textiles, electronics, retail, and construction (OECD, 2022[3]). In these sectors, which accounted for 43% of private employment in 2022, the share of low-skilled employment (both blue and white collar) ranged from almost 60% to over 80% (Figure 3.16). In very few sectors, the share of skilled workers exceeded 50%. They include the education, health and public administration sectors which attracts the majority of Tunisian university graduates and has been an important driver of skilled employment growth. The banking and insurance sector as well as business services are the other main sources of high-skilled employment, representing 10% of private employment.

Figure 3.16. Skills composition of employment in Tunisia

Share of workers by occupation category and by activity, 2017 (in %)

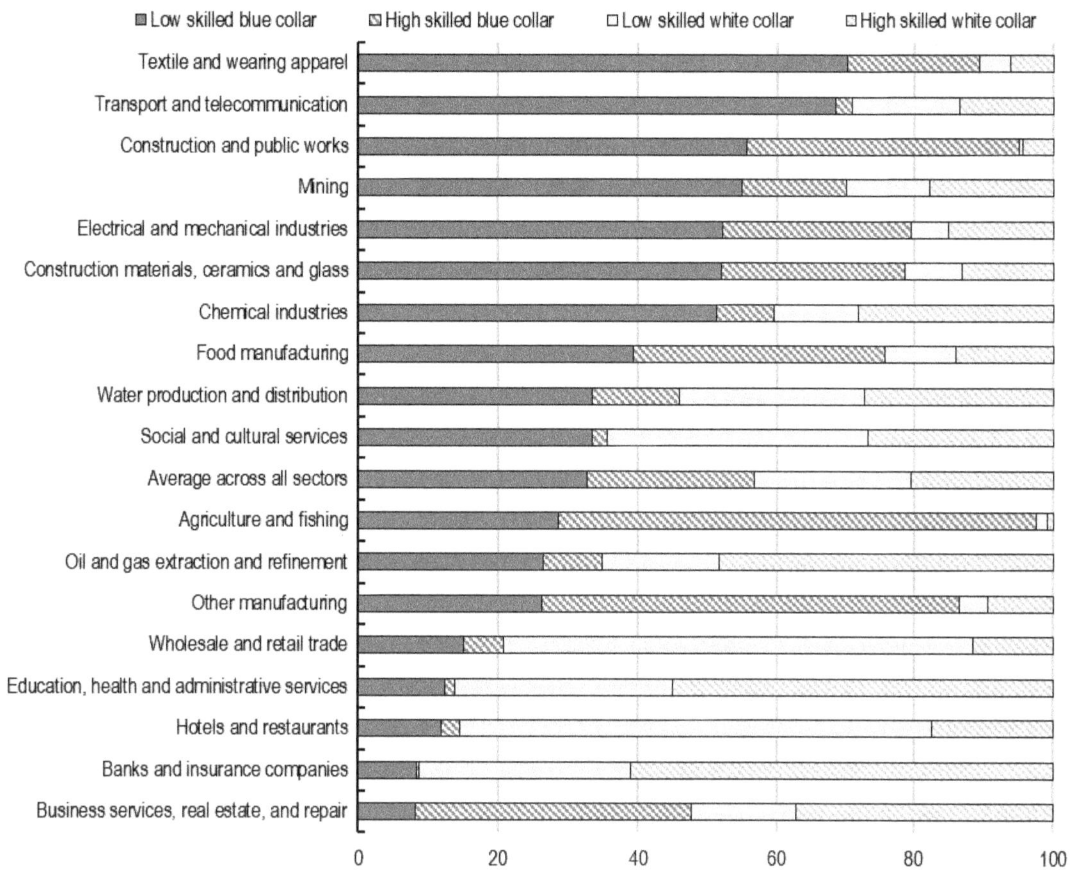

Note: According to the International Standard Classification of Occupations (ISCO 08) low-skilled blue collar workers comprise plant and machine operators and assemblers and elementary occupations. High-skilled blue collar workers include skilled agricultural and fishery workers and craft and related trades workers, whereas low-skilled white collar workers include clerks and service workers and shop and market sales workers. High-skilled white collar workers include legislators, senior officials and managers, professionals as well as technicians and associate professionals.
Source: (OECD, 2022[3]) based on Labour Force Survey of the National Institute of Statistics.

Lower-skilled labour is higher in sectors creating most of the FDI-related jobs. The textile and leather and the electric-electronic sectors account together for 60% of all the new jobs created from FDI during 2013-2022 and half of employment in foreign companies in 2022, but as low-value added industries, they are dominated by low-skilled blue-collar employees (Figure 3.17). Much of the activities in these sectors is based on assembling jobs that require basic skills. Similarly in the mining sector, where one in four firms is foreign, 67% of jobs are low-skilled. The skill-intensive financial services sector, while attracting 10% of FDI during the period 2013 2022, was not an engine of employment growth, as it contributed to less than 1% of new jobs created from FDI (Figure 3.5). There is scope for skills spillovers in the business services sector – another important sector for high-skilled jobs, as one fourth of firms in this sector are foreign. Furthermore, as FDI has been increasingly concentrated in higher-value activities, it has the potential to improve mid- or high-skills demand in some sectors, particularly in electronics.

Figure 3.17. Foreign employment is concentrated in sectors with predominantly low skills

Share of high-skilled workers and foreign share in employment by sector

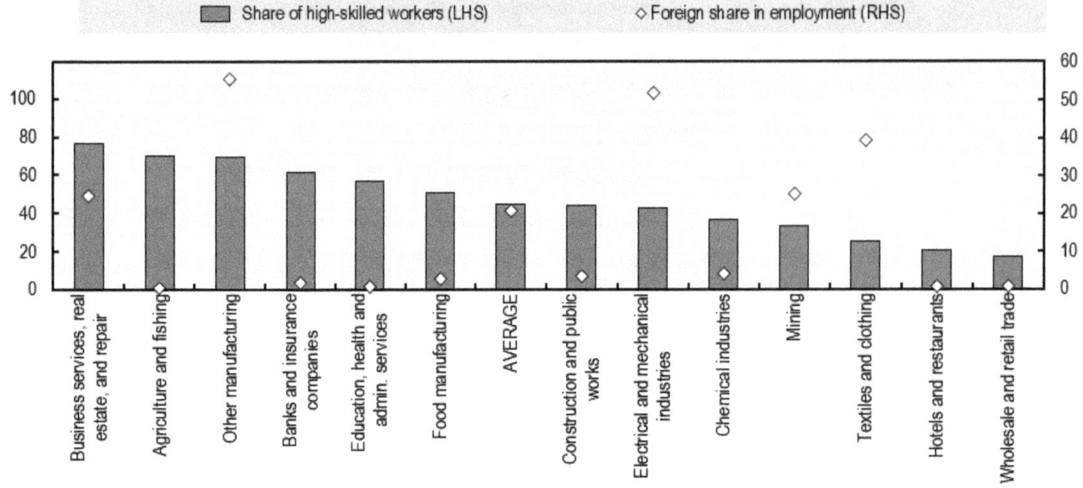

Note: The share of high-skilled workers includes blue collar and white collar workers (see fig. 3.16).
Source: OECD calculations based on (INS, 2023[14]), the Répertoire National des Entreprises (RNE); and (OECD, 2022[3]).

The domination of low-skilled job offers together with high annual numbers of graduates results in skills mismatches on the Tunisian labour market. Skills mismatches occur when workers struggle to find employees with the right skills while job seekers do not find employment that meet their level of qualifications or education. This may be either because companies require advanced skills that are insufficient among workers or on the contrary, potential job seekers are overqualified for the type of jobs that are available on the market. The mismatches not only lead to higher unemployment and lower job satisfaction, but the inefficient allocation of labour is also associated with lower labour productivity (Adalet McGowan and Andrews, 2015[27]).

In Tunisia, the problem of an overqualified workforce is more common than in other MENA countries, resulting in unfilled vacancies despite high youth unemployment (OECD, 2022[28]). Over-education on the job is strongly correlated with age in Tunisia, with the youngest workers being the most affected (Kthiri, 2019[4]). Despite a rapid growth of the educated workforce, especially women, there has been limited employment creation for this group. During the period 2011-2017, the total number of university graduates exceeded by 25% the total employment creation during that period and was six times higher than new jobs in high-end occupations (World Bank, 2022[5]). In view of the lack of opportunities, many young people prefer to stay unemployed and wait for a well-paid and stable government job, emigrate abroad, or even exit the labour market, as is more often the case of women (Boughzala, 2019[2]). In addition, limited labour mobility from more deprived regions to those with more employment opportunities, further contributes to mismatches on the labour market.

As a result of the structural skills imbalances, many more companies in Tunisia than in other MENA and comparable countries are finding it difficult to hire adequately educated workers. Almost 40% of companies identify inadequately skilled workforce as a major constraint (against the MENA average of 20%), with the problem being even more pronounced in foreign firms (Figure 3.18). As many as 44% of foreign companies perceive an inadequately skilled workforce to be a major constraint, in contrast to 34% of domestic firms. Moreover, this share has increased in the past decade, from 34% for foreign firms and 28% for domestic firms in 2013 (World Bank, 2024[25]). Sectors where employers are most likely to have difficulties finding adequately qualified labour include the textiles and leather sector, construction and hotels, and ICT sector, where there is also a high share of foreign firms (ITCEQ, 2018[29]). While skills mismatches are the primary reason for recruitment constraints in Tunisia, other factors identified by firms in Tunisia include high salary expectations and geographical distances (Boughzala, 2019[2]).

Figure 3.18. Firms identifying an inadequately educated workforce as a major constraint

Percentage, 2020 or most recent year available

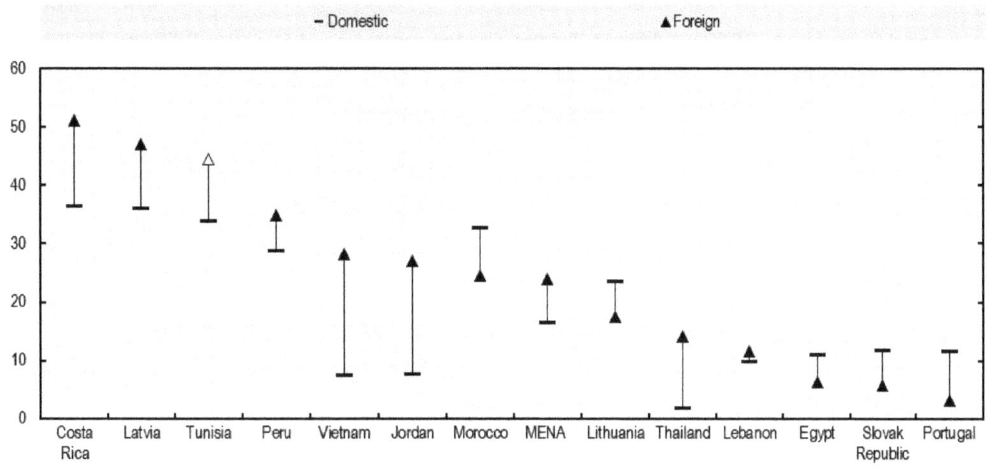

Source: OECD calculations based on (World Bank, 2024[25]), World Bank Enterprise Survey, https://www.enterprisesurveys.org/en/data.

FDI can be an important channel for skills development even if most jobs are concentrated in low-skilled sectors. Foreign firms may contribute to increasing the overall skills supply as they are typically more likely to offer skilled jobs and on-the-job training compared to their domestic counterparts (OECD, 2019[26]). In Tunisia, the employment of skilled workers is relatively low, with only 50% of employers (domestic and foreign equally) hiring skilled workers, in contrast with 76% in the OECD and 73% in the MENA economies (Figure 3.19, panel A). Nevertheless, FDI in less skills-intensive sectors can still bring benefits if firms offer skills upgrading to its workers which improve the overall skills intensity of the workforce. This is the case of Tunisia where foreign firms are twice as likely to offer training to its employees, with 38% of foreign companies providing formal training versus 19% of domestic ones (Figure 3.19, panel B). While this rate is lower than that observed in comparable OECD countries, much more foreign firms in Tunisia provide training than in other MENA economies.

Figure 3.19. Firms hiring skilled workers and offering training

Percentage, 2020 or latest year available

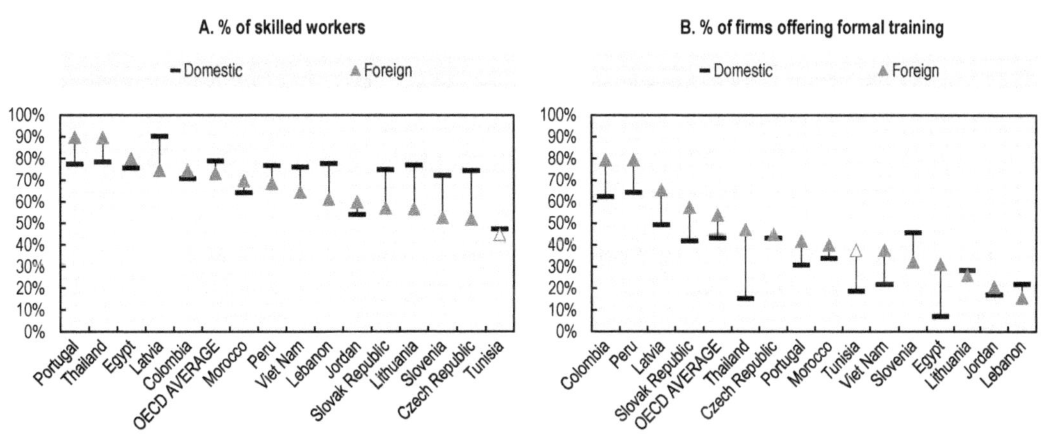

Source: OECD calculations based on (World Bank, 2024[25]), World Bank Enterprise Survey, https://www.enterprisesurveys.org/en/data

References

Adalet McGowan, M. and D. Andrews (2015), "Labour Market Mismatch and Labour Productivity: Evidence from PIAAC Data", *OECD Economics Department Working Papers*, No. 1209, OECD Publishing, Paris, https://doi.org/10.1787/5js1pzx1r2kb-en. [27]

Belgacem, A. and J. Vacher (2023), "Why Is Tunisia's Unemployment So High? Evidence From Policy Factors Approved by Amine Mati", *IMF Working Paper* No. 2023/219, https://ssrn.com/abstract=4619837 (accessed on 6 January 2024). [9]

Boughzala, M. (2019), *MARCHÉ DU TRAVAIL, DYNAMIQUE DES COMPÉTENCES ET POLITIQUES D'EMPLOI EN TUNISIE*, European Training Foundation, https://www.etf.europa.eu/sites/default/files/2019-08/labour_market_tunisia_fr.pdf (accessed on 29 January 2024). [2]

Boughzala, M. and M. Hamdi (2014), "PROMOTING INCLUSIVE GROWTH IN ARAB COUNTRIES RURAL AND REGIONAL DEVELOPMENT AND INEQUALITY IN TUNISIA", *Global Economy & Development*, Vol. Working Paper 71. [11]

Bouzid, B. and S. Toumi (2020), *The Determinants of Regional Foreign Direct Investment and Its Spatial Dependence Evidence from Tunisia*, World Bank Group. [18]

Financial Times (2024), *fDi Markets database*, https://www.fdimarkets.com. [19]

FIPA (2023), *Rapports annuels des IDE*. [16]

ILO (2024), *Labour Force Statistics*, https://ilostat.ilo.org/data/. [6]

ILO (2024), *Statistics on wages*, https://ilostat.ilo.org/topics/wages/. [23]

INS (2024), *Répartition de la population active occupée selon le secteur d'activité*, https://ins.tn/statistiques/151. [10]

INS (2023), *Répertoire National des Entreprises (RNE) database*. [14]

INS (2022), *STATISTIQUES ISSUES DU RÉPERTOIRE NATIONAL DES ENTREPRISES - 12 Edition 2022*. [13]

INS (2020), *Indicateurs sur l'emploi informel 2019*, https://ins.tn/publication/indicateurs-sur-lemploi-informel-2019 (accessed on 26 January 2024). [1]

ITCEQ (2018), *Climat des affaires et compétitivité des entreprises : Résultats de l'enquête 2016*, Institut Tunisien de la Compétitivité et des Etudes Quantitatives, http://www.itceq.tn/files/climat-des-affaires-competitivite/enquete2016-climat-des-affaires-competitivite.pdf (accessed on 1 February 2024). [29]

Kthiri, W. (2019), "Over-education in the Tunisian labour market: Characteristics and determinants", *EMNES Working Paper n.22*, http://www.emnes.org (accessed on 20 March 2024). [4]

Ministère de l'Industrie, D. (2022), *Stratégie Industrielle et d'Innovation 2035*, http://www.tunisieindustrie.gov.tn/si2035/Livrable_7_Rapport_final.pdf. [20]

OECD (2024), *Labour Force Statistics*, https://stats.oecd.org/. [7]

OECD (2023), *Analytical AMNE Database*, https://www.oecd.org/sti/ind/analytical-amne-database.htm. [15]

OECD (2023), *OECD Guidelines for Multinational Enterprises on Responsible Business Conduct*, OECD Publishing, Paris, https://doi.org/10.1787/81f92357-en. [22]

OECD (2022), *FDI Qualities Policy Toolkit*, OECD Publishing, Paris, https://doi.org/10.1787/7ba74100-en. [21]

OECD (2022), *FDI Qualities Review of Jordan: Strengthening Sustainable Investment*, OECD Publishing, Paris, https://doi.org/10.1787/736c77d2-en. [28]

OECD (2022), *OECD Economic Surveys: Tunisia 2022*, OECD Publishing, Paris, https://doi.org/10.1787/7f9459cf-en. [3]

OECD (2022), "The geography of foreign investment in OECD member countries: How investment promotion agencies support regional development", *OECD Business and Finance Policy Papers*, No. 20, OECD Publishing, Paris, https://doi.org/10.1787/1f293a25-en. [17]

OECD (2021), *Middle East and North Africa Investment Policy Perspectives*, OECD Publishing, Paris, https://doi.org/10.1787/6d84ee94-en. [8]

OECD (2019), *FDI Qualities Indicators: Measuring the sustainable development impact of investment*, Paris, https://www.oecd.org/investment/investment-policy/FDI-Qualities-Indicators-Measuring-Sustainable-Development-Impacts.pdf. [24]

OECD (2019), *FDI Qualities Indicators: Measuring the sustainable development impacts of investment*, https://www.oecd.org/investment/investment-policy/FDI-Qualities-Indicators-Measuring-Sustainable-Development-Impacts.pdf. [26]

World Bank (2024), *World Bank Enterprise Surveys*, https://www.enterprisesurveys.org/en/enterprisesurveys. [25]

World Bank (2022), *Tunisia's Jobs Landscape*, World Bank Group. [5]

World Bank (2014), *The Unfinished Revolution: Bringing Opportunity, Good Jobs And Greater Wealth To All Tunisians*, World Bank Group, Washington D.C., https://documents.worldbank.org/en/publication/documents-reports/documentdetail/658461468312323813/the-unfinished-revolution-bringing-opportunity-good-jobs-and-greater-wealth-to-all-tunisians. [12]

www.ingramcontent.com/pod-product-compliance
Lightning Source LLC
Chambersburg PA
CBHW061224240926
51846CB00006B/1346
* 9 7 8 9 2 6 4 6 3 1 6 0 1 *